SHOWELL STYLES
BACKPACKING
A Comprehensive Guide

M

Front endpaper: Free from
road and railway, the
backpacker heads for open
country. Back endpaper:
Only the backpacker can
camp in delectable places
like this one, in the
mountains of Spain. Title
page: Backpacking in
Switzerland gives you the
world-famous views without
the crowds

Acknowledgements

The publishers are grateful to the following for supplying
illustrations:

Bergans: 15tr; Berghaus: 15tL, 18tL; Blacks of Greenock:
29b, 31t, 38t, 50; Brown Best: 15bL; Europleasure International
Ltd: 38b, 45; German Embassy: 77; Bradford Herzog: 58-59; Holubar Ltd: 31b;
Colin V Morgan: 4, 9, 10, 16, 27, 33, 41-42, 46-47, 48, 52, 55, 62, 63, 67, 70t,
74, 79, 84, 86, 94; Harold Morris: 2, 18tr, 18bL, 18br, 23bL, 24br,
25, 27 inset, 29t, 34, 39, 60, 70b, 85; Hester Norris: 69;
Pindisports (John Cleare): 51; Saunders: 23t; Silva Compasses
Ltd; 56, 82; YHA Services Ltd: 15br

SBN 333 18537 4

First published 1976 by
Macmillan London Limited
London and Basingstoke
Associated companies in New York, Toronto,
Dublin, Melbourne, Johannesburg and Delhi

Phototypeset by Yaleset Limited, London
Printed in Great Britain by Shenval Press Limited

Contents

1 What is 'Backpacking'?

You are a backpacker from the moment you set out on a journey carrying on your back everything you need for existence — bed and shelter, food and the means of cooking it, and the minimum comforts you consider necessary to the happy life. Backpacking is the art of travelling independently, of seeing the world (or part of it) without relying on trains, planes, hotels, restaurants, or any of the usual tourist conveniences. True, you may have to use some of these things to reach the starting-point, but during the journey you will be free of the technological society; your only care will be the need to stock up with food every three or four days. You will have to face bad weather and know how to cope with it, to sleep on the ground with only the flimsiest shelter above you, and to carry a weight of twenty-five pounds or more wherever you go. And, since backpackers naturally journey where there are no roads or sign-posts, you will have to know how to find your way. The rewards are great: you can explore the vast and beautiful areas of the world that are closed to the motorist and the house-dweller, and you can make your journey as short or long, as mild or adventurous, as you like. Backpacking is a pastime — even a way of life — that can bring you health and pleasure from childhood to old age. As a holiday sport, it has gained enormous popularity in recent years.

First, a brief note on the history of backpacking. The word originated in America at the time of the pioneers, when trappers and explorers 'backpacked' their way into the untamed wilderness, where pack animals could not be taken. In the pack on their shoulders they carried a blanket or fur robe for sleeping, a bag of flour, powder and shot for their long rifles, and little else. At the time of the Yukon Gold Rush in 1897, backpackers performed prodigious journeys with their heavy loads, crossing high passes like the Chilkoot with packs weighing a hundred pounds or more. When modern America began to conserve her remaining wilder-nesses as national parks, the old trails were opened up again by ad-venturous wanderers journeying in the self-reliant way of the pioneers. Subsequently, backpacking became increasingly popular with Americans of all ages, resulting in the establishment of such magnificent routes as the Pacific Crest Trail, a backpacking journey of 2,313 miles. In Britain, meanwhile, hikers carrying lightweight tents had discovered the delights of long journeys through the mountains and moorlands of their own country. A nationwide campaign to preserve these wild places forever ensured the rapid development of this sport, and the term 'backpacking' was quickly adopted, together with many American ideas about proper equipment.

The equipment you need
Backpacking is a craft as well as a sport. In fact, it is a collection of crafts: you must know how to walk with a heavy load, how to camp, how to cook, and how to follow a route. No craft can be learned without the proper tools. You could just start walking with a bundle, like a tramp, but to extract the utmost enjoyment from your journey you must have certain basic items of equipment.

The only physical requirement is good health. Backpacking can be enjoyed by boys and girls and men and women of all ages. The vitally important thing is for each to see that the equipment

Below: A romantic campsite above the Lotschental, Bernese Oberland

chosen, and (especially) the weight carried, is right for him or her. The items of equipment and how to choose them will be discussed in detail later. You will need proper walking boots, a well-designed rucksack or packframe and sack, a lightweight tent, a sleeping bag, and special outer garments to protect against bad weather, as well as other items, such as a stove, depending on the type of journey you are likely to make. The appendix lists the sort of things that go into a pack.

Types of backpacking

Backpackers have been defined as those who carry in their rucksacks food and the means to prepare it, and shelter for their overnight stop. But so also are the folk who tramp the two-thousand-mile Appalachian Trail (or part of it) and instead of carrying a tent use the shelters that are spaced out along the Trail. Though they carry no shelter themselves they are surely back-packers. I once tramped across Europe from Gloucestershire to Genoa and back, carrying tent and sleeping bag, and my overnight stops included inns, barns, ruined keeps, and a Salvation Army Hostel, as well as fifty-three nights in the tent. Still, I would call it a backpacking journey. And I know one or two hard men who make week-long treks across wild areas without a tent or sleeping bag; they sleep rough in the heather or under the hollow side of a peat-hag, but they are definitely backpackers.

On the other hand, the climbers who carry a lightweight tent to the foot of a remote rockface and camp there for three days' climb-ing can't be called backpackers, nor can Youth Hostellers, in spite of their rucksacks, since they are dependent for cooking and over-night shelter on a succession of hostels. The wandering students, who hitch-hike vast distances, often carry the most enormous packs, but in general they rely on faster forms of transport than their own two feet, and they are not backpackers either.

Two things give a person the right to be called a backpacker: the intention of making a long journey across country where wheeled transport cannot go, and the capability of being entirely self-dependent on that journey. I say 'the capability', because the chan-ces of travel may bring the backpacker a night of storm in a hospitable farmhouse, or a lift on a section of road which connects two parts of the cross-country journey. I don't believe the back-packer forfeits his title if he accepts these fortuitous aids; the im-portant thing is that he should be equipped and ready to do without them. Absolute independence is the true backpacker's ideal, and — when he achieves it — one of his most satisfying rewards.

The scope for backpacking

Never have so many beautiful regions of the world been open to the ordinary man or woman who can walk with a pack. This statement may seem odd in view of the fact that the highways, once busy with walkers as well as with riders and drivers, are now either impossibly dangerous for pedestrians or actually closed to them by law. A hundred years ago the adventurous walker went on a 'walking tour', exploring his own country or others by tramping its highways and byways; he had neither the equipment nor the knowledge for exploring the wilder and quieter places, and he would not likely have gone there if he had. Today, with the roads devoted almost entirely to motor traffic, rapid developments, including the designation of national parks and the establishment of trails and long-distance footpaths, have given the traveller on foot a far better chance of seeing the wonders of his world than ever before.

In terms of distance and area the scope for backpacking journeys is extensive indeed. In the USA the two chief mountain trails total more than four thousand miles of walking, and in Britain there are now fifteen hundred miles of long-distance footpaths, not to mention the shorter backpacking routes to be found in the ten national parks. A summary of the opportunities available to the backpacker in ten countries of the world will be found in Chapter 8.

In another way, too, the scope is wide. The chosen journey can vary from safe and easy to hard and hazardous, with many gradations between the two extremes. For an instance of the 'safe and easy' in Britain, a journey could be planned using the bridleways, field paths, and public footpaths which are well-marked on the new 1:50,000 Ordnance Survey maps, avoiding roads and camping at night but keeping always within reach of inns and other amenities. This sort of journey would be advisable for a backpacking family making a first experimental trip, or for young backpackers with little time and money to spare. At the other end of the scale are some of the European mountain routes which involve crossing precipices clinging on to fixed wire ropes, and the magnificent Pacific Crest Trail in the USA which climbs to more than twelve thousand feet in places. Forest trails in America, moorland and hill-path journeys in Britain, the lower mountain passes of Switzerland and Austria, the rarely-visited glens and cols of Norway — all these provide a great variety of climate and scenery, as well as a wide variation in difficulty.

There are strenuous backpackers who set themselves the task of completing a long journey within a given time, but most backpackers simply want to enjoy a leisurely trip. When they find a place they like, they stay a few nights to explore. In my experience, this is the way you find the life of freedom and independence which backpacking, more than any other pastime, can give.

2 The Pack

This all-important item of the backpacker's equipment has undergone many changes and developments in the last few years. Not so long ago, you simply bought the biggest rucksack you could find and filled it with everything you needed, but new ideas and designs now appear on the market every month or so, and the range of models is bewildering. Modern theory is almost entirely in favour of the packframe, a separate frame of aluminium or light alloy tubing on which the sack is slung. The packframe is American in origin, based on the wooden Yukon packframe invented by the trappers and prospectors of the Northwest a hundred years ago. Variations are beginning to appear, such as pneumatic pack supports, and frames made of reinforced plastics and polypropylene, and it may well be that in a year or two some quite new design will appear.

The newcomer to backpacking, faced with the problem of buying a pack, should remember that the habitual heavy-load carriers of the world use widely different methods, none of which include a packframe. I have seen a Sherpa carry a hundred-pound bundle on his back using a length of rope round its base attached to a headband resting across his forehead; Chinese peasants sling two balancing loads on each end of a bamboo pole borne on one shoulder; Africans carry big loads balanced on their heads. All these methods require the development of certain muscles to take the strain, and the cultivation of a new balance in walking. So does the packframe, however well-designed it is. When you add thirty pounds to your normal weight, there is no apparatus (despite the claims of some advertisers) that can make the carrying of that extra load pleasant and comfortable, until your muscles have adjusted to it.

This doesn't mean that any old sack will do for your backpacking journey. You are not a habitual heavy-load carrier and for your holiday jaunt you need a pack that will quickly become bearable; moreover, modern packs have gadgets and conveniences specially designed for the sort of load you will carry. The important thing to remember is that the latest and most expensive packframe might be totally unsuitable for you and your needs. The human frame is infinitely variable, in proportions and muscles and posture, and there is no ideal packframe suitable for everyone. Before acquiring a pack, then, consider first your requirements and then spend as

Above left: A typical packframe (Berghaus's 'Mach 4'). Above right: One of the bigger frames loaded with pack and sleeping bag (Bergans 750 Viking). Below left: Medium-sized nylon pack on medium frame (Brown Best's Super Loadstar). Weight unloaded 3lbs 4oz. Below right: YHA Super Highpack. A conventional rucksack-type pack made in proofed canvas

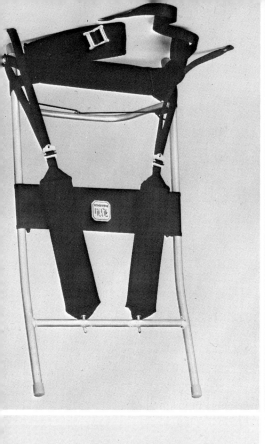
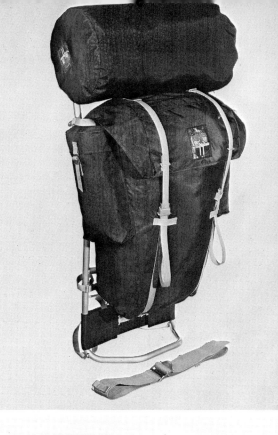
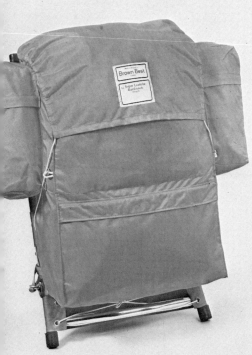

much time and trouble as you can afford in testing many likely models.

Requirements

You probably have some idea of the sort of backpacking journeys you intend to make. Suit your sack to that idea. The solo walker needs a big sack for full-scale backpacking because he carries a complete tent and cooking apparatus; the two inseparable companions can do with smaller packs because they share out those things between them. It sounds a good idea to start with one of the big frames, that extend way above your head, so that you can sling small or large sacks on it as required, but large packframes are a nuisance both on the trail and off it, no matter how good they may be for carrying huge loads between camps in the Himalayas. In woodland, they catch on every branch, you can't get them in the tent at night, and in bus, train or car they are a great inconvenience to all.

Above: Packframe with high-slung sack and carrying-bar below. A sleeping bag in a thoroughly waterproof container could be strapped to the carrying-bar, but the tent should be carried on top of the load

Estimate, if you can, the top limit of weight you are likely to carry. There are backpackers who value comfort and good living on the march far above petty considerations of weight, and these will gladly suffer a forty-pound burden; others delight in existing on bare essentials and refuse to carry more than twenty-five pounds. For an average man, thirty-five pounds is a top limit. I try to keep my own pack-weight down to twenty-five pounds excluding food; with five pounds of food, and the stripped-off clothing I shall carry on top of the sack on a hot day, I shall have quite enough of a burden.

American backpackers consider that any weight over twenty-five pounds can best be carried with a packframe. I would question this. On backpacking journeys across the Alps and the Pyrenees totalling ten weeks, I carried thirty to thirty-five pounds in a rucksack-type sack (YHA *Super Highpack*) which is now in its fifth year and ready for further journeys. The compact load had many advantages and was the envy of my big-frame companions.

When you come to chcose your sack, therefore, consider the uses you will put it to, the weight you are likely to carry, and whether the advantages of a packframe will exceed the disadvantages.

Choosing a pack

By all means get to know all about the latest packs and frames. The catalogues of the equipment suppliers and the advertisements in outdoor magazines such as *The Climber and Rambler* in Britain or *Summit* in the USA will give you a good look at what is currently available. But never buy a pack or frame by mail order without having seen it. By far the best and safest way to choose a pack is to wear and, if possible, carry for some distance, laden packs made by several different manufacturers. This sort of trial can be managed without much difficulty if you are a member of a walking

Above: Windproof cagoule attached to pack with press-button straps. Below: Large and medium packs in the Pyrenees. Note the stockings drying out on the packs

or climbing club, and much can be learned from it:

1 Compare the effect of two well-loaded sacks on your balance when standing and walking; one may drag you off your normal balance more than another, and if so it is either a badly designed pack or wrongly packed.

2 When buying a packframe, check that the lower crossbar does not chafe your spine.

3 Beware of shoulder straps made of material so light that they fold to half width.

4 Check the wide padded waist-harness found on many recent models. The body's pelvic frame is better able to bear weight than the shoulder bones, and this padded harness, strapped tightly, transfers seventy-five per cent of the burden from shoulders to hips. However, those with slim hips may find this system un-comfortable and prefer to carry the weight on their shoulders.

If you are not able to make this sort of trial, the alternative is to go to the biggest local equipment store and try on a variety of the packs available. Insist on having heavy weights in the sack and walking up the store staircase. Of course, it won't be as effective a trial as walking miles across country wearing the sack fully loaded, but it's better than nothing; and since you may be paying £25 ($60) or more, the bother is worth it.

Remember that comfort in use is the most important criterion for the pack you choose. Other important things — material, good workmanship and so on — are irrelevant if you acquire a pack that is going to irritate you throughout your journey.

Material and workmanship

The choice of material for the sack presents the sort of problem that crops up with protective clothing. You naturally want your sack to be waterproof, and waterproof nylon keeps all wet out most efficiently. But its very efficiency leads to trouble inside the sack; the material can't breathe, so the slightest dampness of con-tents condenses and spreads. Water-repellent nylon duck, on the other hand, allows minor dampness to escape and so prevents this nuisance; but it won't stand up to a real downpour going on for hours, when everything in the sack will get soaked. Both sorts of nylon are more liable to get accidentally ripped or damaged by abrasion than cotton duck, which is tougher and also allows the sack contents to breathe; but cotton duck is heavy, and heavier still when its proofing fails to withstand heavy rain. In all three cases, the counter-treatment is to use individual plastic bags for the contents, which is a good way of keeping your belongings in order anyway. For my own part, and bearing in mind the hard treatment a pack has to suffer in trains, planes and luggage-trailers, I prefer heavy-duty proofed cotton duck. However, if you have a cotton sack you must make sure it isn't put away damp, or you will

be inviting mildew.

Examine a sack for sound workmanship before you buy it:

1 Check nylon material for nicks, tears and abrasions.

2 Look for good reinforcement at all points of stress; especially the part on which the laden sack will rest when lowered to the ground.

3 See that straps, buckles and zips work easily. I don't like zips myself, but if fitted they should be nylon zips on nylon material, metal zips on cotton duck.

4 If you are buying a packframe, separate from the sack, take a good look at the frame joints and check the whole frame for rigidity. The maker will have given a curve to the lower crossbar of the frame; make sure it curves clear of your spine.

Pockets and gadgets

Tastes in pockets and other attachments to the outside of the sack vary enormously. Much depends on the additional hobbies of the backpacker: a man walking the high snow passes of the Alps will want a carrying-loop and strap for his ice axe, a photographer will demand several handy pockets for his cameras and lenses, and a sketching addict needs at least one large pocket for his block and pencils. Essentially, there should be two good deep side-pockets for the things you are likely to want out at short halts: map, compass, and a little food. These pockets should be at least six inches wide, to take the map or maps in use, and have big fully-overlapping tops. Because I can never remember which is the right- or left-hand pocket when I've taken the sack off, I label the port (left) red and the starboard (right) green, keeping the route-finding apparatus in starboard and the sweets and chocolate in port.

It is always a nuisance to have objects suspended about the exterior of a sack, but an exception can be made with protective clothing — weatherproof cagoule and trousers. These may need to be donned very quickly and without having to open the top of the sack, which would let in the rain. I haven't come across a pack with a built-in provision for this, but a simple 'do-it-yourself' job can solve the problem: two light straps sewn on each side, between the side-pockets and the body, with press-stud fastenings, hold the weatherproofs on my sack. If the flap of the sack is a properly large one and has long straps, any other clothing likely to be needed on the day's trip can be strapped under the flap.

3 Boots and Clothing

For backpacking, boots are essential — neither shoes nor plimsolls can be substituted. The man with the big pack on his back and plimsolls on his feet may be on a round-the-world vacation trip but it's obvious that he isn't going to walk any farther than he has to. For comfort, support, and safety on awkward trails, the real backpacker wears good boots and cares for them as if they were his best friends — which, on a journey, they are. The man who thinks he can manage without boots on a backpack journey doesn't understand his own feet.

Care of the feet
Your feet are delicately adjusted mechanisms of small bones, conditioned to work according to your body's weight and your personal habits of standing and walking. It is unlikely that these habits include picking up and carrying an extra thirty pounds whenever you move about. So, when you start backpacking, these delicate mechanisms must suddenly work under an extra load for long periods of time. They will adjust very quickly — if you give them the help they need. The bones require extra support, and the sole — slapped down at every step with additional weight — needs a good padding beneath it. Boots provide both. They don't have to be heavy mountaineering boots, but they must be stoutly made and the sole must be at least half an inch thick. A pair of such boots will weigh between three and four pounds, and if you are not used to wearing boots your feet may become very sore even if the boots are a good fit. You may have no trouble at all; some people have harder feet than others. But before going on to the boot itself let's consider the treatment of the foot that is to wear it.

Really soft feet can be conditioned to boots by daily rubbing with alcohol. Methylated spirits or surgical spirits will do — don't waste the whisky. Test them first, though, by walking with the boots on; wear them about the house for a few days (if you're allowed to), then go out for short walks, increasing the length of the walk bit by bit. If your feet fail to accommodate themselves quite soon, start the alcohol treatment.

On feet new to boots, blisters may form. Here you need something which is going to be an essential part of your backpacking kit: moleskin. Moleskin is a thin adhesive felt that can be put over the blister to ease the chafing at that point. For bad blisters, or when the skin is broken, it is wiser to stop wearing the boot until the damage has healed.

For most people, however, a careful choice of boots will prevent any foot trouble afterwards.

Boots and socks

The first rule is never to buy boots without trying them on. Wear two pairs of socks, wool if possible and in any case with more wool than nylon in the mixture. Remember, when choosing boots, that one manufacturer's size 8 can be smaller than another's; go by the 'feel' on your foot. Here are the points to look for, and feel for, in a new boot:

1 Full grain (unsplit leather) uppers
2 No toecap, no exposed stitching on welt
3 *Vibram*-type soles, lugged all round
4 Toes must be able to 'scrunch up' in the boot
5 Little toe must be able to lie flat inside sole
6 The boot should fit snugly, firm but not hard-pinching, at the broadest width of the foot and have slightly more room at the front and back. To gauge this, unlace the boot all the way down, stand up, and push the toes forward until they touch the end. If you can now just manage to slide your forefinger down into the gap at the heel, the fit is about right.
7 Unlined boots are best, but an inch or so of leather lining making a 'roll-over' on the top rim of the uppers is a good thing.
8 Preferably, there should be two lace eyelets or lugs nearest the toe, then hooks for the rest of the lacing.

As with a new pack, it is not really possible to tell what new boots will feel like until after the first few days of hard use. It might conceivably happen that the boots that felt fine in the shop turn out to be tight in the wrong places after all. There's a remedy for this which I've used more than once, and though it's not too good for the boots, it works: lace the boots as tightly as possible over two pairs of socks, find the boggiest bit of country you can, and walk all day with wet boots. Afterwards, dry them slowly (never dry boots in heat) and rub *Dubbin* into the leather while it's still damp. Some folk prefer to use wax. It's good policy in any case to wax boots as soon as they're bought. Wax should be re-applied sparingly in summer, but more often in winter, especially after a soaking in bogs or snow.

Clothing

Underclothes These should never be of nylon or other man-made fabrics. Cotton garments of the cellular type are best; they are efficient in hot or cold conditions and easy to wash. One set of spares carried in the sack is usually enough. String vests are admirable for keeping body temperature even, but they are most uncomfortable when wet and take a long time to dry. On a backpacking journey it is most important to dry all wet clothes and equipment very quickly. It is essential to take at least one change of socks and stockings because these woollen items may take a day or more to dry after washing.

Top clothes When choosing shirt, trousers etc, you should bear in mind that you will also be carrying a complete weatherproof outer shell. There is little point in using a heavy anorak-type jacket if you have a waterproof cagoule to go on top, or in wearing thick shower-proof breeches if you are carrying overtrousers which are windproof and rainproof, unless, of course, you are doing a winter backpack, which requires a rethink of all equipment. A good thick shirt of wool or flannel which can be opened down the front is good. Jeans are usually too tight-fitting to be worn backpacking; loose clothing on legs is best whether it's hot or cold weather. Personally I prefer fairly lightweight breeches with a good bag at the knee. A pair of very light shorts substitutes for these when the day is fine and warm. Shirt, breeches/trousers, and shorts are all easier to keep reasonably smart if they are dark in colour. So is the sweater you carry for putting on at halts, in camp, or to warm up in. This, of course, should be a woollen sweater, and for summer backpacking, a lightweight one is good enough. Backpacking through the Alps and camping at eight thousand feet, after crossing passes of nearly ten thousand feet, I found a good woollen sweater weighing twelve ounces adequate for all occasions. Spring and autumn tramping can require something thicker, but a heavy knitted sweater may weigh twenty-one ounces or more and take up a lot of room in the pack. Over the shirt, a hiking (or golf) jacket of *Ventile* or similar close-weave cloth, with a zip all the way down the front, is a useful thing to wear, especially if it has plenty of zipped pockets. I use a self-lined *Nomad* jacket (Bertram Dudley and Son, Cleckheaton, Yorks) and find its six zipped pockets very useful when shopping for fresh supplies in town or village. Some people don't like hats, and the hood of the cagoule is efficient enough in driving rain. The broad-brimmed hat has its merits, though, and is essential for summer backpacking in high mountain terrain; it can be slung on the pack, when not in use, by a leather thong passing through two holes in the brim. Pyjamas are sneered at by some backpackers but I always carry them, packed in a completely waterproof polythene bag. They constitute a complete overall change of clothes, and the pyjama jacket can serve as a spare shirt.

Protective overclothing

A knee-length cagoule without zip-front or pouch pocket, and a pair of roomy overtrousers, both of waterproof nylon, give you all-over protecton from rain, snow, and wind. A sack or slipover made

Above: An over-all nylon cagoule can protect the pack as well as the backpacker (Pakjak). Below left: Protective clothing. Cagoule and overtrousers weigh only 27 oz and give complete protection from rain and wind. Below right: Overtrousers with an 11 in zip in the lower leg can be pulled on easily over boots

of good quality waterproofed nylon can be used to protect the pack. The *Pakjak* (Robert Saunders & Co, Chigwell, Essex) is tailored to slip over the backpacker *and* his pack, however large. It weighs only eleven ounces and hangs well below the knees, but you would need to wear overtrousers under it when walking in rain.

The snag with all completely waterproof outer clothing is that body-heat condenses on the inner surface and makes you damp all over. There is no 'breathing cloth', allowing the moisture to escape, which will not let the wet in if it rains long and hard enough. However, it is better to keep the cold rain out and suffer warm wetness than to let in the rain in order to avoid perspiring. So you should choose a nylon cagoule with a polyurethane inner coating, making sure that the hood can be secured tightly round the face and throat and is roomy enough to take a wool balaclava or knitted cap under it for cold-weather journeys. A great deal of discomfort will be saved if you get overtrousers with short zips up the outside of the lower legs; these will make it easy and quick to pull the trousers on over your boots. Overtrousers usually tie round the waist with a cord, which tends to restrict ventilation and add to the interior dampness. If they have a band of openwork material just below the drawcord so much the better — it helps to reduce condensation. There are many makes of cagoule and overtrousers to choose from, all of them satisfactory but varying in length, type of fastening, and so on. I would choose a medium-weight proofed nylon, not the heavy grade; my own outfit, cagoule and trousers (Helly Hansen) weighs twenty-seven ounces altogether and is always carried outside the rucksack, as described in Chapter 2. The zipped access slits at both sides of my cagoule (for getting to pockets) were not much use when wearing overtrousers, which tie above the pockets, so I contrived slits in the seams of the overtrousers as well. This operation has no effect on the waterproofing efficiency and allows me to get at my pockets without taking down my overtrousers.

Polyurethane proofing won't last forever, but its effective life is prolonged by care of the garments. When not travelling, hang them up on coat-hangers in an airy place. At campsites, don't leave them bundled up on the sack; shake them out and pile them loosely. I have often found it a good idea to slip on overtrousers in camp, when the evening air gets chill.

Spares and extras

A saying of George Bernard Shaw's is particularly applicable to the backpacker: 'The more a man possesses over and above what he uses, the more careworn he becomes.' If you take all the spares you think you might possibly need, you'll want a second pack and a porter. One spare set of underwear may be considered essential and should be adequate. One change of socks and stockings is also enough, but of course you should carry darning-needle and wool in the little cloth roll called a hussif (housewife) which also contains

Right: The useful 'hussif'

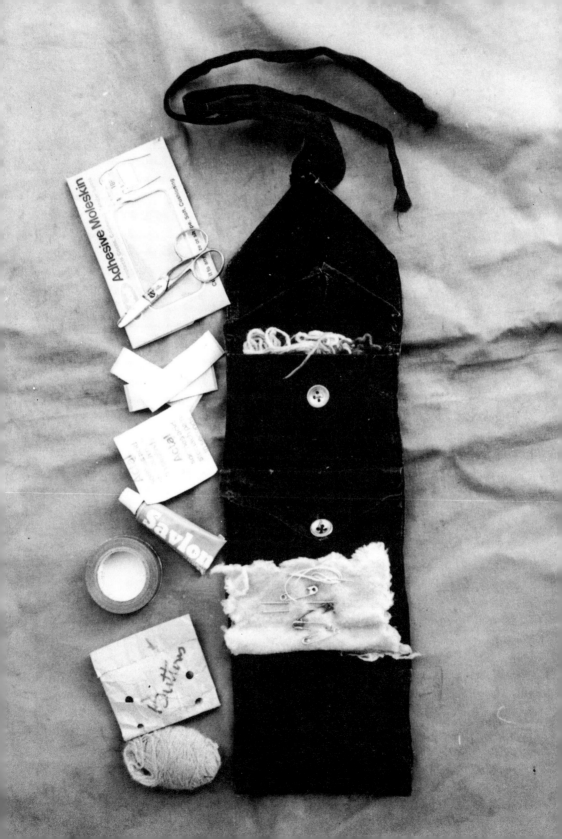

needle, thread, and buttons. In my hussif I include safety-pins, finger bandages, moleskin, a small tube of antiseptic, scissors, a few indigestion and laxative tablets, and a roll of self-adhesive pvc tape for temporary tent repairs. All other small odds-and-ends go in the ditty-bag, a little home-made bag with drawstring top. A large coloured handkerchief (bandanna) has innumerable uses — as a scarf, head-covering, spare belt, emergency first-aid, or top cover for a pillow. A change of shoes for wearing about camp is very nearly an essential, though ultra-lightweight travellers will scorn them. I've found a pair of galoshes (if you can get them) very handy for trotting about in cold wet grass, but they are inclined to be heavy; a pair of moccasins, weighing about eight ounces, would be as good.

Right: On a backpacking traverse of the Bernese Oberland a staff makes for sure footing with a heavy load. Inset: A staff is also invaluable for balance in descending steep paths

The route you propose to take on your journey affects some of the spares to be carried. On the traverse of the Valais passes mentioned in Chapter 8 for example, a pair of windproof mitts might be worth taking. Waterproof gaiters are extremely useful on a route where you expect to do a lot of trudging through snow. Some backpackers use them for keeping out the rain, but I would not bother with them for that purpose alone. Basic for backpacking in cold latitudes or in winter conditions are the additions of gloves, wool balaclava, double-texture jacket or anorak, and extra thick sweater. On winter hills, it is vital to carry an ice-axe if there's *any* snow to be seen.

Soap and toothbrush should be kept in a waterproof sponge-bag. A three-by-two rough cotton towel is big enough; two tape loops sewn on the corners of one end allow it to be dried on the march, slung on the back of the pack. A nailbrush is a desirable extra for the backpacker who likes to be presentable, and a razor, the plastic, bonded-blade sort, for the man who wants to go on looking clean-shaven.

The staff

A staff cannot be considered a basic part of backpacking equipment but, in my own experience, it's an invaluable aid on any journey over rough tracks or steep terrain. Its prime value is in ensuring even balance and steady rhythm on such terrain, and for this a mere three-foot twig will be better than nothing; if it is a stout stick it can help enormously in crossing streams, steep inclines, scree or snow. On all my journeys, my companions and I have cut ourselves staffs from a handy thicket at the earliest opportunity and found them much too useful to part with until the end of the last day's trek. I haven't come across a British supplier of backpacking equipment who stocks staffs, but some American suppliers have them.

4 Tent, Sleeping Bag and Mattress

The tent that is suitable for all kinds of camping, and the sleeping bag that is ideal for everyone, do not exist. But in Britain, the USA and France, the range of tents and sleeping bags now being produced is so extensive that the choice is wide. Before choosing, get hold of all the equipment catalogues you can; they will bring you up-to-date with current developments and show you the variations in weight and price. Examine several different tents and bags if you are able to visit a store. Though both tent and bag are essentials of backpacking, it isn't as important to test before buying as it is when selecting pack and boots. It would be impossible to discuss the merits and deficiencies of all the available models of tent; the most useful method of assisting your choice is to consider the basic points to look for and consider in a solo and a two-man tent.

The solo tent

Before you decide to remain a 'loner' and go for a one-man tent, remember that a change of ideas (such as marrying another backpacker) will mean buying a larger tent; a couple carrying solo tents is uneconomical as well as unsociable. Remember, too, that bad weather may force you to *live* in the tent for a day, and consider, before choosing, what each model will be like when you have to cook in it with rain lashing down outside.

There are solo tents weighing as little as two pounds six ounces, such as the *Backpacker One-Man* (Robert Saunders). These are adequate as shelters and could certainly tempt the backpacker who puts weight first. If you go for a tent of this type, be sure it has a cooking shelter like the *Solite,* developed by Mike Marriott; it weighs three pounds two ounces. The Marriott *Paklite* is a two-man tent of the same design, weighing four pounds two ounces. Such ultra-lightweight tents are always made of nylon. As well as the obvious limit on space, they have the disadvantages of nylon, which include a tendency to leak at the seam joining tent to groundsheet. The *U-8 Bivouac* tent, made by Ultimate Equipment and popular in both Britain and the USA, has this trouble but is otherwise a good minimal design, with its wedge shape and inverted-U poles which give extra headroom. It weighs three pounds and packs to 10 x 8 x 2 inches. When buying any lightweight nylon tent, check that the groundsheet is made of heavier-grade material than the tent, and

Above right: The author's home-designed one-man tent, made in 1938 and still usable today. Below right: Nylon one-man and two-man tents — Solite (left) and Paklite (right). Note the useful cooking shelters

that the flysheet, if fitted, comes right 'down-to-earth' all round, as in the Marriott tents.

For some people, the disadvantages of nylon tents may cancel out their definite advantage of lightness. Nylon tents have, in my experience, a certain flimsiness which means they can't be stretched as taut as other tent fabrics, and consequently flap when there's any wind. A windy night in a nylon tent is invariably noisier than in a proofed cotton one, especially if the wind can get under the flysheet and flap it against the inner tent. Nylon, fully proofed, is impervious to moisture and 'sweats' with condensation inside the tent. To counter this, some tents (including the three mentioned above) have a lightly-proofed inner tent and a fully-proofed flysheet; it doesn't entirely cure the condensation, but it helps a lot.

Going ultra-lightweight involves using the slanting-ridge and tapering-floor design: the tent slants down from a three and a half foot pole at the front to a height of less than two feet at the back, and narrows from about three and a half feet in width at the front to under two feet at the foot. The one-man tent I designed for myself was of this plan, and though it's the lightest design, it has inescapable disadvantages. One disadvantage is that it's nearly impossible to keep the bottom of the sleeping bag dry when it's blowing and raining outside; for this reason, I would never choose a two-man tent with a narrowed floor at the foot. Another disadvantage is that the ridge sags and flaps, a nuisance only prevented by a ridge-tent having an even height and two equal poles. A tent of this narrowed design does have a low wind-resistance, however, and will stand bad weather in exposed places if it is pitched tail-to-wind.

Though nylon is the popular material at the moment, there are also good proofed cotton tents of this narrowed design. An example is the Vango *Force Ten Mk 2*, lightweight grade, which weighs six and a half pounds with flysheet. However, if you decide that comfort in camp makes the extra weight worthwhile, you should look at the roomier designs. A rectangular floor with 'walls' at the foot of the sloping sides gives vastly more living-space than the slanting-ridge design. One example from many is Blacks' *Good Companions Minor,* which has a floor area of six and a half by four feet and a height of four feet at centre. This weighs eight and a half pounds complete with angle poles and pegs, and a solo camper could have all his gear and packframe inside with him and still have plenty of room to sit up comfortably and cook inside the tent. Two people could use this as a single-skin tent (without flysheet) if they were careful campers, of average height and bulk, and using medium-size packs.

All one-man tents currently available have sewn-in groundsheets, and this feature should be regarded as essential for any backpacking tent. Angle poles, mentioned above, are poles of inverted-V shape placed outside the tent, which is then suspended from the apex. Angle poles add as much as three pounds to the

Above right: A nylon tent with flysheet for one man or two weighing 6lb 11oz (Blacks' Oregon 107). Below right: The Holubar 'Chateau II', a backpacking tent from the US

weight but make more space inside the tent. I prefer a single pole inside the tent, not only because it weighs less but also because it makes pitching simpler and provides a safe support for a candle.

The two-man tent

With two-man tents, nylon once again has an easy victory in the weight race. The *Okstinden,* small model, for example, weighs three pounds five ounces, while the higher and roomier *Oregon 107* (Blacks) weighs six pounds eleven ounces. Both use the slanting-ridge, tapering-floor design, as does the Marriott *Paklite.* American tent designers have produced very similar ranges of lightweight tents, among which is the exceptionally rigid Holubar *Chateau* tent, a tapering-floor tent in nylon with a front width of seven feet, a front height of five and a half feet, and a length of ten feet five inches. With poles and flysheet it weighs just under seven pounds. The flysheet, however, loses a lot of efficiency by not being 'down-to-earth'.

Personally, I would look among the proofed cotton tents for a good single-skin model when thinking of backpacking with a companion, bearing in mind that all the camping equipment will be shared out according to weight. (A four-man backpacking party would of course carry two two-man tents.) A flysheet is in many ways a nuisance; the backpacker will quite often want to pitch very quickly indeed to get inside out of the rain, and having to fix a flysheet is then an exasperating chore. Also, a flysheet can weigh half the total weight of tent and poles and it is one more bulky bundle in the pack. If you choose a single-skin tent, make sure that the fabric is a really good proofed cotton, and that the tent is roomy enough for the occupants to avoid rubbing against the fabric during prolonged rain.

When I changed from solo to two-man backpacking, I resolved that my new tent should not weigh more than ten pounds, all-in. This narrowed the field quite a bit. Blacks' *Good Companions Standard,* with single pole, tips the scale at eight and a half pounds, but I wasn't satisfied with the oblong floor shape (7 x 5 ft); I prefer a square floor. The same makers produce the *Itisa Senior,* weighing nine and three-quarter pounds, with a five and a half foot centre pole and a floor six and a half feet square. The material, *Protex 3,* was of proved excellence. This was the tent I bought. It has a couple of minor failings: I like to ventilate a tent by opening the upper part of the door, and you can't do this with a zip fastening; also, the blue colour makes the interior dark in daylight. But over four years, it has stood up to the severest tests and I wouldn't swap it; it looks as if it will last forever anyway. On one occasion, my companion and I were caught by a violent storm at eight thousand feet in the Bernese Oberland. We pitched the tent in one and a quarter minutes (thanks to the single centre pole) and bundled inside just as a two-hour rainstorm began, flailing the tent before a gale of wind. The fierce beat of the rain induced a second

or two of very fine spray through the fabric, after which we stayed perfectly dry throughout the storm, while surface water flowed harmlessly under the sewn-in groundsheet. The centre height of five and a half feet gives real living comfort and I have camped and cooked in the tent, with three of us inside.

Care of the tent

Proofed nylon tents suffer if left for long periods tightly folded or rolled. The more heavily proofed groundsheet tends to suffer most. If possible, therefore, store the tent when not in use by hanging it loosely in a dry place. Damp doesn't affect nylon as it does cotton, so there is no danger of mildew. When using the tent, be particularly careful to avoid bringing it into contact with anything sharp — twigs, barbed wire, rocks or corners of walls — and see that the ground on which it is pitched is free from sharp points. Nylon must never come in contact with hot surfaces.

Proofed cotton tents tend to become affected by mildew if packed and left when they are even slightly wet. When you return from a backpacking holiday, seize the first opportunity of giving the tent a thorough airing. It can then be stored in its bag, rolled as loosely as possible, though it should be brought out and erected occasionally to ensure that the fabric is kept free from damp. If it has to be packed wet on the march, a halt to dry it out when the sun breaks through is worthwhile; a wet cotton tent holds moisture more than a nylon one and is consequently heavier.

A tent with a single centre
pole is the easiest for a solo
backpacker to pitch. (1) Peg
out the sewn-in groundsheet
(left). (2) Erect the pole
(top). (3) Peg out the guys at
your leisure (above)

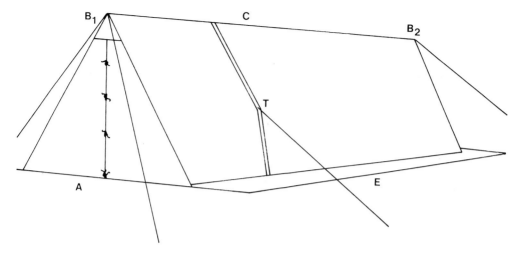

Making your own one-man tent

A backpacking tent can be made at home, given a modicum of handiness with a needle, the use of a sewing-machine, and some patience; it's a job for those long winter evenings. My own tent was designed with minimum dimensions for a solo camper using sites on mountain tops. The cutting patterns can be drawn from the following specifications:

Above: Home-made solo tent. A — door end 4ft wide, 3ft high. B¹, B² — poles, two guys to each. C — slanting ridge 7ft 6in. T — extensor guy. E — extended groundsheet, 8in sides and rear. Below: Types of sleeping bag quilting

Interior length: 7ft
Height at front: 3ft
Height at foot: 14in
Width at front: 4ft
Width at foot: 18in
Fabric: *Protex 3* (originally proofed Sea Island cotton)
Groundsheet: *Wavelock* nylon-supported PVC, sewn-in, extending 8in outside at sides and foot
Doors: 6in double flap, tape tied, with bottoms tucking into a sleeve along the front of the groundsheet
Pole: 2-jointed bamboo; a 14in stick used at the foot
Ridge: strong webbing double-sewn on, ringed at each end to take pole and guys
Extensor guys: double-sewn strong braid on walls 14in from front, D-rings for guys attached 20in down from ridge
Ventilator hood: a 7in equilateral extended by the front guys
Pegs: 12 light alloy pegs, round section
Weight: including all the above, 3lb 14oz

Protex and *Wavelock* material can be obtained from Blacks of Greenock. This tent is efficient as a shelter; otherwise, the disadvantages that go with the slanting-ridge, tapering-floor design apply to it. Nevertheless, I have camped with it on the summits of the fourteen Welsh peaks over three thousand feet, and cooked in it

cold air penetrates

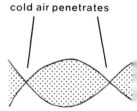

simple quilting: unsatisfactory

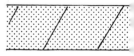

walled quilting: good

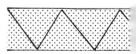

overlapping tube quilting: best, but means extra weight

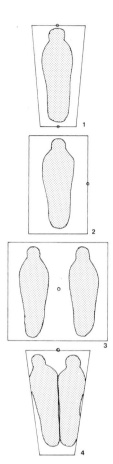

too. Making this tent will cost about one-third of the price of a similar tent chosen from the catalogues.

The sleeping bag

For the average backpacking journey, a medium-weight, medium-priced bag is good enough for most people. The expensive 'mummy' bags, filled with top-quality down, are excellent for Arctic or Himalayan travel, but are wasted on a summer holiday, even when the route lies through mountains. On the other hand, cheap bags that use fillings of man-made fibre give poor warmth value in relation to their weight. The backpacker's sleeping bag should weigh no more than four pounds and cost under £10 ($22) at present (1975) rates. There are many good makes in this class.

Down is the best filling and down-and-feather is second-best. Down takes in and retains the heat from the body, thus keeping you warm; but it does this only if it can expand or fluff out freely within its quilted compartments, so it follows that the compressed down beneath you as you lie in the bag is doing little to warm you. Fillings of man-made fibres like dacron don't compress as easily as down, but they produce less warmth. A bag that makes the best of both fillings is the *Viking* (Blacks) which uses dacron in the underside and a high-quality natural plumage filling on top. It weighs three pounds six ounces. This is the sleeping bag I use, and though it is satisfactory in most ways, it is only six feet three inches long. For a person of average height, I consider six and a half feet a minimum. Heat loss is greater from the head than from any other part of the body, and though this is usually a boon (otherwise you would often be too warm in a sleeping-bag), you need to be able to get your head down into the bag when the night is cold. Quilted hoods and 'mummy' tops add to the weight and bulk of the bag. With a bag that's too short you could use a woollen cap. A zip at the side of the sleeping bag is a great help for getting in and out or for cooling down, but a long zip lessens the effective warmth of the bag and an eighteen-inch zip (which should be nylon, not metal) is enough.

When buying a sleeping bag, make quite sure that the covers are not stitched quilt-fashion, as the stitching between the down-filled compartments makes thin places where the cold can get in and the warmth escape. The bag should have walled quilting, or overlapping tube quilting. Cambric is better than nylon for the cover; the down must be allowed to disperse the moisture given off by your body.

Care of the sleeping bag

The makers will tell you whether your bag can be washed or whether it should be dry-cleaned. However, washing can ruin a bag and dry-cleaning can spoil it. A sleeping bag should need neither if it is properly looked after. A washable sheet lining can be used, although this is one more thing to carry and is unnecessary if

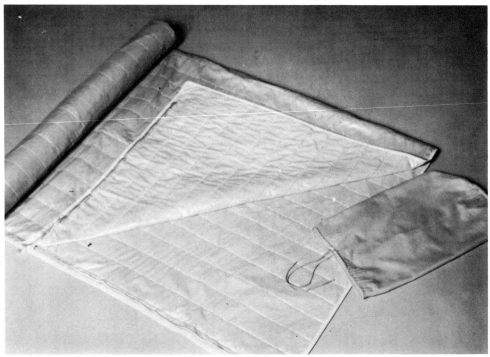

Above left: Viking sleeping bag with 18in zip. Below left: A sleeping bag for the 'hardman' backpacker who puts light weight before warmth — the Polywarm lightweight, weighing only 28oz. Not recommended for cold temperatures. Above: Some form of insulation from the ground is essential. This sealed foam-rubber ground mat (Karrimat) weighs only 8½oz

you wash your feet after the day's journey and wear pyjamas. It is important to dry the bag out thoroughly at the earliest opportunity if it gets the least bit damp. Every morning, or as soon as weather permits, it should be turned inside out and spread carefully on dry rocks or bushes to air.

The mattress

Sleeping bag and groundsheet alone will not keep the cold from spreading up from the ground into your body. Heather and even bracken beneath the groundsheet are better than nothing, but the wise backpacker always carries some sort of mattress. A hip-length air mattress weighs two and a half pounds, and though it is efficient, I consider it too heavy. Ground mats of sealed foam-rubber like the British *Karrimat* or the American *Ensolite* weigh far less and are good insulation, though they do little to cushion you on hard ground. A friend of mine discovered one solution: a child's inflatable boat called a *Surfrider,* which weighs only six ounces and cushions from hip to shoulder, as well as providing perfect insulation. When folded, it took up scarcely any space in the pack. Experiments of this kind are certainly worthwhile!

5 Food and Fire

There are campers who insist on cooking the sort of meals they are used to having at home, and though this may be fine for a standing camp to which the food, utensils, and a large stove have been transported by car, it would be foolish to try for this kind of eating on a backpacking journey. The records of Arctic and Himalayan expeditions, as well as all the doctors, tell us that we can live on a fraction of what most of us usually eat — and live more energetically, too. In my experience I have found this to be perfectly true. A backpacking journey is a holiday from ordinary life, so it should be a holiday from ordinary eating.

The backpacker's menu
Much depends on the country through which your journey is going to be made. You may pass through a town every couple of days and be able to stock up with anything you fancy, or you may go for a week without encountering any supply place except a tiny mountain hamlet where they sell nothing but bread and wine. The key to maintaining a satisfactory menu is to carry certain basic foods with you in small quantities, replenishing this reserve whenever the chance offers, and making up the rest of the meals with whatever you can obtain on the way. It's unlikely that you will make more than three camps between one supply point and the next, and bread is one of the things you can expect to get in any place where people live. A most important basic food is packet soup, of the Knorr-Swiss or Maggi type. With this in reserve you're sure of a hot supper even if your only other food is a last crust of bread. Another basic is sugar, needed in extra quantities by anyone using a lot of energy and best eaten on the march in the form of chocolate and sweets or glucose tablets, which give a quicker energy boost. Salt is another basic, a physical necessity after a hard day's backpacking. Either tea (in teabags) or instant coffee is important; liquid in more than normal quantity is one of the backpacker's chief needs.

Secondary foods, to be carried and replenished as opportunity serves, are eggs, butter, and cheese. Third come the desirable luxuries like jam, fruit, tomatoes, and sweet biscuits, bought in a local store as you go along. On a long journey fruit should be eaten whenever possible to keep up your vitamin quota, but its food value doesn't compensate for its heavy weight and the prudent backpacker eats it on the spot or at the first halt. Milk is another common commodity to be drunk when available but not to be carried. For those who *must* have milk in their tea, a milk powder can be carried.

To summarize these suggestions:

(1) Permanent reserve in each pack: 3 packet soups, sugar, salt, teabags or small tin of instant coffee

(2) Basic foods from stocking-up points: bread, eggs (4 to each person), butter, cheese, chocolate and sweets

(3) Additional luxuries: jam, sweet biscuits. Fruit, tomatoes, milk, consumed en route when possible.

The backpacking menu on this basis will be:

Breakfast: boiled egg, bread, butter, and jam, tea or coffee

Lunch (wayside): bread, butter, and cheese, tomato, sweet biscuits, chocolate

Supper: hot soup with plenty of salt, bread and butter, sweet biscuits and jam, tea or coffee

Apart from the modest variety afforded by the different flavours of packet soups, the evening meal can be varied by adding things out of tins, like ravioli. Tinned food is rarely worth carrying for three days and weight-watching backpackers will eat it in the first camp after stocking-up. For some a tin of fruit salad (its weight nearly all water) is worth carrying as far as the first halt for lunch, for its refreshing qualities.

Concentrated meal packs like those supplied for backpackers by Springlow (see Appendix) simplify cooking and eating even further but tend to be more expensive. Some folk may consider the packet-soup-based diet deficient in bulk or protein, but my companions and I used it in 1972, 1973, and 1974 on three long European journeys, one of them lasting four weeks, and on each occasion we all finished very fit and lost our fitness only when we returned to normal eating habits.

Carrying food supplies

The plastic bag and the rubber band are invaluable aids for carrying some items of food. Packet soups are normally well sealed but the reserve packets could open a crack after a fortnight's bashing in the pack so they should be kept in a plastic bag. For carrying sugar I use a polythene bottle with a screw top, nine fluid ounce size; you pour out the sugar instead of using a spoon. Salt and coffee can go in similar containers of suitable size, but teabags need a waterproof box or stiff plastic bag. If you are travelling with a companion and you both have a sweet tooth it makes for harmony if each carries his own sugar. A four-man backpacking party (two tents) works well if each tent-pair does its own stocking up and sharing of food-weight.

Butter (a main source of fat) and cheese (a main source of protein) are always a problem to carry. One solution is to use a stiff plastic lunch-box, with a lid that makes a positive seal, and store

Overleaf: A woodland campsite a few yards off the track. Stoves can be done without in this sort of country.

the butter in its wrapper in one end and the cheese, in polythene, in the other. A rubber band keeps the box closed in the pack, where it should be carried wrapped in a spare sweater if the day is hot. A butter box with supplies for two can be carried by one person, while the other carries the bread. Loaves of bread vary in size, shape, and weight, but the handiest are the loaves of 'black bread', often circular, which you find in the remoter country districts of Europe; they are close-grained, hard, nourishing and keep well. There is really no way of carrying long French loaves except under the flap of the rucksack. Eggs are safely carried in the four-compartment egg boxes obtainable wherever camp equipment is sold; each person in the party should carry a four-egg box. Chocolate and sweets are personal stores which should be carried in jacket pockets or accessible side-pockets of the pack. It's quite astonishing how nibbling these at frequent intervals can maintain your energy on the day's march.

Of the luxuries, jam is a valuable source of the much-needed carbohydrates but is usually sold in a heavy glass container. Jam in tins invariably means a sticky mess in the pack unless you eat the contents at one go. A plastic jar with a good tight lid is the best solution. Sweet biscuits contain as much as seventy-five per cent carbohydrates and, like jam, count as a 'necessary luxury' for the backpacker. They generally come in long packets, and much wastage by crumbling in your pack can be saved if you choose packets with stiff cardboard down the sides. The only safe way to carry a tomato (refreshing for the wayside lunch) is in the drinking-mug.

Stoves

The most efficient stove for camp cookery or 'brew-up' is still the *Primus,* which uses paraffin under pressure. The *Primus 210* will boil a quart of water in five minutes, even in a breeze. But I've never succeeded in carrying a paraffin stove without being haunted by the smell, which seems to get into everything; it invariably gets on your fingers when you're operating the stove. Moreover, liquid fuel has to be carried, which is always a nuisance. Petrol stoves (for example, the *Optimus No 111B*) are efficient too, but involve the same awkwardness of carrying reserve petrol. Solid fuel such as *Meta* avoids this difficulty but is much less efficient as a quick heat-producer. Still, the *Meta 71* stove starts with the great advantage of weighing only three and a quarter ounces, complete with fitted billy holding just over half a pint, and it is absolutely clean to use. It takes fourteen minutes and two bars of solid fuel to boil half a pint of water, with enough heat left to boil an egg, so the solo backpacker travelling ultra-light and content with an egg and soup or coffee as the hot courses of his meal could manage with this very small outfit. However, it has to be remembered that solid fuel works well only in draught-free conditions.

The stoves using *Camping Gaz, Go-Gaz,* or *Veritas* score over

Left: Meta solid-fuel stove with fitting half-pint billy and lid. Right: The Bleuet S.200 stove using propane gas. Overleaf: One of the many good moments on a backpacking journey — when the pack becomes a pillow

the liquid-fuel stoves because they are perfectly clean in operation and reserve fuel cartridges can safely be tucked into the pack anywhere. However, they are rather expensive to operate. A *Camping Gaz* cartridge won't last more than one and a half hours, and the flame takes longer to boil a billy of water than the *Primus* does. But the refill cartridges are usually obtainable throughout the holiday areas of Europe and the USA, and this form of stove is the most convenient for the backpacker. The most popular model is the *Bleuet S200.* It weighs twenty-two ounces with its cartridge in position and packs to nine by three and a half inches. By comparison with the *Meta 71,* it boils half a pint of water in four and a half minutes. The folding base supplied with it is of little use except on a perfectly level floor; it is safer to use the stove with the

45

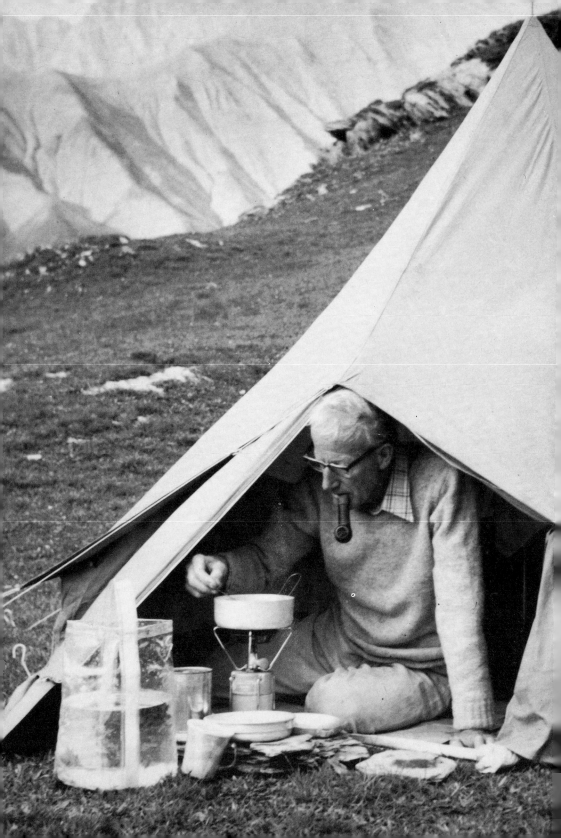

base in a hole scooped in the ground, or propped round with rocks. Using a *Bleuet S200* on two of three recent mountain journeys we found that a three-camp stretch used approximately one and a half cartridges per two-man tent. A spare cartridge was always carried by each pair of backpackers. The gas tap of the *Bleuet* needs to be tightened very firmly before packing, so that friction in the pack doesn't cause it to loosen and release gas.

A much lighter stove is the *S7000 Ultra-Light Camping Stove* (Vango). It weighs only six ounces without cartridge. However, its system involves a length of flexible tubing between stove and cartridge, and this doubles the risk of upsetting, especially when cooking inside the tent.

Fires

In places where stove fuel is not easily replaceable, cooking on a camp fire may be necessary, and though it involves extra work and blackened utensils, you do get heating as well as cooking facilities at no cost. Wood for fuel has to be available, of course, either at or near the campsite, and you should make sure before starting that you are not breaking any forestry regulations.

I used fires at every camp for four weeks in the Pyrenees, partly because gas cartridges were unobtainable in Spanish mountain villages, and partly because there was an abundance of wood

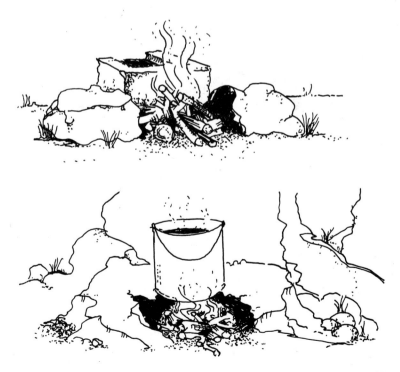

Left: Cooking the soup on a Bleuet S.200. The flame needs some shelter from wandering breezes. Right: The backpacker's fireplaces

everywhere, especially pinewood and that best of firewoods, juniper. The secret of camp cooking on a wood fire is to take trouble to select dry small wood to start the fire and to build the smallest fire compatible with getting a good continuous flame. After rain, the driest twigs are to be found clear of the ground, broken-off pieces lodged in the lower branches of trees or thickets, for example. It is sound practice, involving very little extra weight, to carry a few small dry pieces of wood in case the fire has to be started in the wet.

Before building a wood fire, a simple fireplace has to be constructed. On open ground or on level wooded sites, the 'Sherpa' fireplace usually works well. Three large stones are placed so that the edge of the billy will rest securely on all of them, leaving three spaces between. These supports should raise the billy at least six inches from the ground. When the fire of small sticks is well started it is fed by pushing larger dry sticks in through the three openings. In mountainous country, the vertical face of a large boulder or small cliff can be used for the fireback, with two rocks, flat on their inner sides, pushed close against the face so that the billy will bridge them. If there are any gaps between the rocks and the fire-back they should be plugged with turf to give a good draught. Care must always be taken to keep fires under control, particularly when the ground is dry.

Above: Folding polythene water-bottle. Right: With the primus paraffin stove outdoor cooking presents no problems

Utensils

The frypan is an article many backpackers manage to do without; the carrying of an extra item, plus the cooking-fat, added to the chore of cleaning the pan afterwards, usually cancel the pleasures of a fry-up. A two-man backpacking party basing their meals on my recommended 'backpacker's menu' would take two billies, one of one and a half pint capacity, for soup, and one of one pint, for tea, coffee, or egg-boiling. The smaller billy nests inside the larger one and the handles are saucepan-type, detachable. When using wood fires for cooking a lid is advisable for both billies unless you like your tea smoked and your soup flavoured with wood ash. Fire cookery will also require a light cloth bag, with drawstring, to contain the blackened pots when packed.

Cutlery for each person includes a dessert spoon, two teaspoons, and a knife. A large and sharp sheath knife or hunting knife should be carried for bread-cutting, as well as for trimming that invaluable staff. One large plate should suffice for each, but it should be deep enough to hold soup. A double-skin plastic picnic mug is best for hot drinks; metal mugs tend to burn the lips. The can-opener must not be forgotten; and if your celebratory bottle is going to be vintage wine you will need a corkscrew as well.

Recent backpacking journeys have led me to believe that a collapsable one-gallon water bottle is a 'must'. It weighs only four ounces, folds small, and is absolutely invaluable when the water supply is some distance from the tent.

6 Finding the Way

Wherever your backpacking journey takes you, it will probably steer clear of signposted roads, and you may be travelling a route where you can't count on meeting someone who will tell you the way. Even if your route follows lanes and bridle-paths, there will be forks and crossways. Left, right, or straight on? If you take a chance you may go miles off course. In short, you need a map.

A map, however clear and accurate, can only show you how the land lies in relation to other landmarks shown on the map. It can't show how it lies in relation to you. You may learn from it that the woodland path you are following bends northward and that just beyond the bend you must look out for a smaller path heading north-east. But to locate the northward bend, or to check that the smaller path is taking you in the right direction, you need a compass.

Map and compass, and the basic knowledge of how to use them, are backpacking essentials.

The map

Britain, most European countries, and the USA produce maps on the scale of 1:50,000, which is two centimetres to one kilometre or approximately one and a quarter inches to one mile. This is the map the backpacker needs for his journey. The British Ordnance Survey maps on this scale can be obtained through most bookshops and stationers; on these maps the routes the backpacker is most likely to use — hill tracks, footpaths, and bridle-ways — are marked in red dots or dashes when they are public rights of way. If the journey is to be in Europe and a map is required for advance planning, a good source of supply is The Map House, 54 Beauchamp Place, London SW3 1NY. Many regions popular with walking tourists produce special maps showing the walking paths, with marked routes to huts and passes, and official campsites. These can usually be obtained only in the region being visited, from the office of the local tourist organisation, the *Syndicat d'Initiatif* in France or the *Verkehrsverein* in Germany. They are limited in scope and are supplementary to the essential 1:50,000 map. Details of maps for the USA are given in Chapter 8.

Your map is more than just an aid to route-finding; it is packed with information about the countryside you're walking through, and provides a means of identifying every river, mountain, lake, or town you come in sight of. The British Ordnance Survey maps always contain a key to the conventional signs, instructions on how to pinpoint a spot anywhere on the map by means of a grid reference, and a diagram showing the differences in angle between Grid North, True North, and Magnetic North. Continental and other maps do not give all this information, but the 1:50,000 European maps state the compass-direction differences in words, in the bottom border of the map. Grid North, which is in effect the North to which the parallel sides of the map point, varies slightly from True North because the map has to represent part of the

world's curved surface on a flat surface. The difference in angle between True North and Magnetic North varies in different parts of the world and must be taken into account when the compass is used for route-finding.

The Compass

Your compass need not be one of the expensive models, but it should be one of the type that is mounted on an oblong base of transparent plastic. The *Silva* is the most popular compass of this kind, but the *Suunto,* made in Finland, is also very good. A compass usually comes with a pamphlet giving the most detailed and exhaustive information on how to use it for various purposes, but the ordinary backpacker need only know the basic uses; the method can be summarized quite simply.

First, note the variation (stated on the map) between True North and Compass or Magnetic North. For general route-finding with British maps, this can safely be taken as ten degrees; the red end of the compass needle points about ten degrees *west* of True North, as indicated by the sides and vertical grid lines of the map. This must always be taken into account when steering courses or taking bearings.

Now, imagine that you are on a high trackless moor with thick mist hiding everything and you want to get safely down to a village three miles away. Lay the open map flat and place the compass on it so that the long side of the oblong base is parallel to a straight line joining your own position on the map to that of the village; the arrow engraved on the base must be at the end nearest your destination. Next, turn the movable ring of the dial until the engraved lines inside the circle are exactly parallel to the vertical grid lines of the map, with 'N' for North uppermost. Read off the number where the arrow-line on the base cuts the edge of the ring. That figure is the *True* bearing which you would follow to reach the village, but because the magnetic needle is to be used to guide you you must now correct it to the *Magnetic* bearing. Since Magnetic North is west of True North, and to correct for a westerly variation you always *add* (for an easterly variation you *subtract*), you must now add the difference of ten degrees. For example, if your arrow-line cuts the ring at the figure 80, add 10 and turn the ring until the arrow cuts it at 90. Finally, turn the whole compass until the needle points exactly to 'N' on the dial. The arrow now points straight to the village you want to reach, and all you have to do is to keep the needle steadily pointing to North while you walk in the direction in which the arrow points.

The most important requirement for this operation is that you know your own position. This is something the backpacker in open country is continually checking; it is essential to establish your position on the map before mist or cloud blots out your surroundings. This done, and your destination known, map and compass will guide you safely.

Probably the commonest use of the compass for the backpacker is in checking that he is on the right path. He looks at the map to see which direction he ought to be going, takes out the compass and holds it so that the needle points to the angle of variation from True North, and checks the direction of the path. Sometimes it is useful to take a bearing of a distant object — to identify a mountain peak, for example. The simplest way of doing this is to turn the movable ring until the needle points to the variation from True North, and then, holding the ring steady in that position, turn the base until the arrow points to the mountain. Read off the number on the ring, which gives the True or Map Bearing of the mountain from your position. Transfer that line of bearing to the map and it will pass through the peak.

Lastly, here is an exercise by which you can test your compass-work before setting out on a journey. Go to the nearest grassy open space, taking your compass and a coin. Well out in the field, place the coin in the grass. Then, using the compass, walk twenty-five steady, even paces on True bearing 45 (NE). Halt. Walk twenty-five paces on True bearing 135 (SE). Halt. Walk seventy paces on True bearing 270 (W). Now pick up your coin. If you find it within ten feet of where you finish you've not done badly!

Waymarking

On backpackers' routes across mountains and high moors in Britain there is no standard form of waymarking. There is strong (and quite reasonable) opposition to waymarking on British hills

Below: Silva compass, 'Orienteer' model. Overleaf: Selecting the onward route over pathless terrain in the Pyrenees

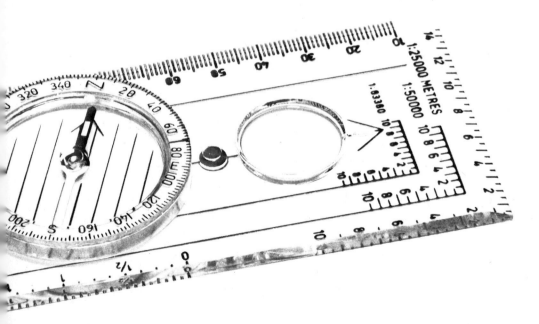

since the areas where genuine route-finding with map and compass can be practised are very limited. Cairns — small piles of stones — are used to mark the more frequented hill routes, but these routes are nowadays well-beaten tracks which are easy to follow in clear weather. In mist, however, you have only to stray a few yards from the path to be adrift on trackless ground which holds the possibility of danger; and since mist is one of the commonest hazards on the high ground of Britain no walker with any sense ever starts on a hill journey without map and compass. In the lower terrain of enclosures and farmlands, stick to routes marked by the *Public Footpath* signs, or if you want to cross a farmer's fields or pasture ask his permission first. Almost without exception, farmers and landowners anywhere are fierce if they catch you on their land without permission, but ready to grant it if you ask. Naturally, you must close all gates, leave no litter of any kind, and avoid climbing over walls and fences; if you have to climb over a padlocked gate, climb it close to the hinges.

On the continent of Europe, waymarking is the rule rather than the exception. France is using a red and white waymark on the recent extensions of the network of ramblers' paths, and in Germany and Austria many centres differentiate walking routes in wilder country by using paint of a different colour for each route. Switzerland is in the process of standardizing the waymarking system on the Alpine paths; yellow marks indicate the lower and easier walking routes, red and white marks signify a *Bergweg* or mountain route. If you're journeying in the Alps and want to use a *Bergweg,* get information about it first from the local tourist bureau; some *Bergwegs* cross high, difficult or snowy ground. The trails in the USA are nearly all well waymarked with metal tags, small cairns, and tree-blazes in forests.

Never rely on waymarking and a map alone; the compass should always be your final safeguard. Crossing a high, well waymarked pass in the Valais, my companions and I found deep snow lying in the upper section in early August. Waymarks across this tricky part of the route had been painted on boulders at intervals of two or three hundred yards — but they were below the level of the snow. Without the compass we could not have found our way.

Above: If you have to cross a stone wall, look for a stile or proper way over

Orienteering

Apart from its importance for backpacking, the craft of finding your way with map and compass is worth acquiring for its own sake. It's very satisfying to know that you can travel anywhere in the world without getting lost. The best way of becoming really skilled in the craft is to take up orienteering, which uses map and compass as the tools of an exciting sport. Orienteering has become immensely popular in a remarkably short time; as well as local meets, there are now international competitions at frequent intervals. Hostelling or rambling associations will be able to put you in touch with your nearest orienteering club.

7 A Backpacker's Day

At seven o'clock in the morning the backpacker was awake in his tent, lying in his sleeping bag and staring up at the tent roof. There was a little condensation moisture on the fabric, which meant that it had been a fairly cold night, but a good sleeping bag and insulation from his foam-rubber ground mat had kept him warm. This was the tenth morning of his solo backpacking journey; he had another four days of holiday to come. For the first time on his journey the tent was pitched on an official campsite. The rain of the previous day, catching him as he came down from the hills towards the town in the valley, had made him decide to use the campsite instead of camping above the cultivated areas as he usually did.

He undid the short zip at the side of his bag and sat up for a stretch. Not for the first time, he blessed the roominess of his single-skin tent, which allowed him plenty of freedom sitting up and made it easy to avoid rubbing against the wet fabric. It had also allowed him to spread his waterproof outer garments loosely over the packframe beside him, so that the quick-drying nylon was fit to put on over his pyjamas. He got himself into the waterproofs, pulled boots on, and ducked out of the tent doorway. It was a cloudy morning but not raining; the grass and the tent were still wet. He'd have to pack a wet tent, because even if the sun came out it wouldn't strike the place where he was pitched until late in the morning.

That was one of the disadvantages of an official site: you had to pitch where you could among a lot of other campers, instead of choosing the best site as you did when camping wild. Also the ground under your tent had usually been beaten hard by previous users and the grass was worn down to the bare earth, which meant mud when it rained; the underside of his sewn-in groundsheet would need a wash after the night's rain. Still, it made a change to have the use of regular conveniences and a tap and basin for a wash.

Back at the tent, he poured water into his billy from the polythene water bottle which he had topped up the night before. The morning was quite windless, and fast brightening, so he stood the little butane gas stove just outside the tent and put the billy on the flame before going into the tent to get dressed. The previous night he had laid out everything he would need for breakfast, so that if it had been raining hard in the morning he could have cooked and eaten inside the tent — without getting out of the sleeping bag, even. And it was to be a luxury breakfast. He had arrived before the shops closed the day before and as soon as the tent was pitched he had bought enough supplies for a three-night trek; the plastic shopping bag, which weighed three ounces and took up scarcely any room in the pack, came in handy for this. In addition to his usual camping food, he had bought a carton of milk and the smallest available packet of *muesli,* so he was able to begin his breakfast with cereal and milk while his egg was boiling.

The widespread rumour that drinking the water that eggs are boiled in gives you warts inside meant nothing to this backpacker, who had done just that for years. Coffee (for once with milk) was made as soon as the egg was out of the billy; he had allowed enough water so that some was left over for washing up. Through the open door of the tent he could now see a patch of blue sky; it was going to be a good day. He decided to start at eight-thirty, and had a look at the map. The footpath he wanted to follow, to cross the hills into the next valley, started from a point two miles up a lane running north-west from the main road through the town; and he could reach that lane by the bridle-track passing the back of the campsite. After that there was a good eight miles of rough going on hillside and moorland to reach the next village, but he would camp somewhere before the village, perhaps fairly high in the hills where the streams would be pure and the views excellent.

Below: An 'official' campsite at Gsteig, on a traverse of the Bernese Oberland. Right: Backpackers leaving a Spanish village after 'stocking-up' for a three-camp journey

After the washing up, there was the packing to be done. The wet ground gave no chance of airing the sleeping bag and pyjamas so the backpacker gave them a good shaking outside the tent, turning the bag inside out. With the rest of his clothing, these were packed low in the sack, since they were lightweight for their bulk. Heavy high, light low; in loading the pack he always followed this wise rule. Map, compass, and sweets for eating en route went into one side-pocket; into the other went his drinking-mug, which was chosen so that it would fit, and into the mug went a tomato for lunch. Above the spare clothing in its plastic bags he packed stove and utensils, also in plastic bags, with basic food supplies on top of these. Spare sweater and lunch box went in last. Cagoule and overtrousers were rolled and secured to the outside of the rucksack with the press-button straps he had fitted himself. Now the only things left were the bags for the tent pegs, the pole, and the tent itself. He put the tent bag into the top of the sack (no use packing a wet tent in it) and went round with the peg-bag pulling up pegs, counting them as he did so and wiping them clean; there were sixteen. With the spares and the three pole-guy pegs that still held the pole erect that made twenty-two — the proper total. The tent was collapsed, and the joints of the pole went into their bag. He shook as much of the wet from the tent as he could before folding it so that the muddy underside of the groundsheet did not transfer dirt to the rest of the tent fabric. Then he rolled the tent and strapped the tent and pole-bag under the big top flap of his sack, with the plastic shopping bag below them to stop any drips from getting through the laced-up mouth of the sack. He had paid the site fee the night before, so there was only one more thing to do: a last careful look round his tent site for the smallest bit of litter. Then he shouldered his heavy pack, grasped his ash staff, and walked out of the campsite, dropping his litter bag into the camp garbage can as he passed it.

Within an hour the backpacker was clear of houses and lanes and a fold of the hillside cut him off from the sounds of the road in the valley. Overhead there was a blue sky. He greeted a pair of walkers, resting beside the steep track, and smugly noted that after ten days' backpacking he could make better going uphill with a pack than ordinary folk without one!

The hillside grew steeper and more rugged; he sucked sweets as he climbed to renew the energy he was using up. The sun was shining and a brisk breeze was blowing; just right for drying out the tent. However, that would be a longish job and better left until lunchtime. Under the brow of a ridge he halted for five minutes, choosing a place where he could support the base of the pack on a steep little bank and thus wriggle easily out of the straps — and back into them when the time came to move on. From his position he could see across the valley to the hills he had crossed the day before. After a nibble of chocolate, he put on the pack again. Soon he was on the high moorland of the ridge, where bright streams

good

bad

hopeless

on hard ground

Above: Pegging in

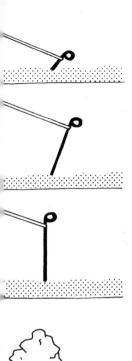

came down through heather and boulders, foaming high after the rain of the day before. Since our backpacker had had breakfast at seven-thirty, he had lunch at noon; he never went as long as five hours on a backpacking journey without a meal and the rest that went with it. A short distance across the tall heather from the track was a spot where a stream came over a little fall between grey rocks, with a clear pool below. Here he made his lunchtime halt, again finding a rock where his pack would rest ready to be put on without effort.

The wet tent came first. He spread it out across a smooth grey slab of rock close to the stream and managed to swab off the worst of the mud from the groundsheet. Then he slung it loosely on the heather to dry in the sun, and looked for a comfortable seat. The plastic shopping bag came in handy, forming the base of his chair on the damp ground, with the woollen sweater folded in it as cushion and insulation. Lounging with his back against a sun-warmed rock, munching bread and cheese and tomato and drinking sparkling water from the stream, he wouldn't have changed places with a millionaire dining at the Dorchester or the Ritz. He got up after ten minutes or so to turn the tent (the groundsheet dried off very quickly) and let the fabric dry; after that he shifted the cloth at intervals to speed the work of sun and breeze. Altogether he spent nearly an hour in this pleasant spot — pressing on at speed was not what backpacking was about, to his mind. By this time the tent was nicely dry. He rolled it and put it into the tent bag, with the poles and pegs, and after shouldering his pack he went on.

Through the first part of the sunny afternoon the path wound its way over uneven moorland of rock and bog; there were few distinctive landmarks near or far. From time to time the backpacker checked his direction with his compass, and twice he stopped to get out the map and establish his position on it. The path was clear enough across hard ground but tended to vanish where it crossed marshy patches; here he was careful to find the path again and ensure with the compass that it was the right one. It was after three o'clock when the moorland streams were running in the same direction as he was, downhill, and before long he could see the far ridges beyond the still invisible valley ahead of him. Away to the right, below a heathery crag, a stream ended its small cascade by curling peacefully across a little green strath bordered by rocks. 'The perfect campsite', he thought, 'if that strath is dry ground and well above stream-level'. He left the path to reconnoitre. It was a perfect site. Not only was it dry and reasonably smooth; it also sloped very slightly towards the east, was sheltered from the prevailing westerly winds, and had handy boulders for airing clothes and sleeping bag.

The time was three forty-five, which was early for pitching camp, but our backpacker knew from long experience that a good site underfoot was worth ten hypothetical sites farther on, and in

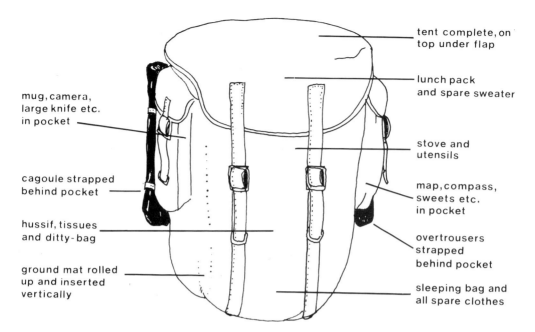

mug, camera,
large knife etc.
in pocket

cagoule strapped
behind pocket

hussif, tissues
and ditty-bag

ground mat rolled
up and inserted
vertically

tent complete, on
top under flap

lunch pack
and spare sweater

stove and
utensils

map, compass,
sweets etc.
in pocket

overtrousers
strapped
behind pocket

sleeping bag and
all spare clothes

any case he always started looking for a site before five o'clock. He off-packed then and there and cast a keen eye over the ground, choosing with deliberation the best ground for the tent: slanting slightly from rear to front, not too near the noise of the stream but not too far away, a place where the sun would strike as soon as it topped the distant hills in the morning. Up went the tent. It was an easy job; he pegged out the groundsheet and erected the centre pole, which stood up by itself while he positioned the other pegs and guys. There was stony ground under the turf, so he carried one or two hefty rocks to strengthen the pegs that wouldn't go in far enough. The next job was to unpack and get out the sleeping bag, which hadn't received a proper airing that morning. Shaken up and turned inside out, it was spread on a dry boulder to make the best of the remaining afternoon sunshine. This done, the time had come for a brew-up.

This particular backpacker wasn't a luxury camper but he liked tea at teatime and coffee for breakfast, so he carried teabags. Being an economical soul, he had experimented to discover which brand of teabag gave the best cuppa, and had found one which produced two cups of good-strength tea from one bag (the secret, alas, he never divulged). A nook at the base of the crag sheltered the stove from wandering breezes and in a few minutes he was reclining in the sun and enjoying a good brew. A late pitch, he was thinking, never gave you enough time for this sort of thing. There'd be time, here, to have a good look round, to scramble to the top of the heathery crag, to explore a bit farther down the stream.

He did all these things, to his great enjoyment. But the exploring

Above: 'Heavy high, light low'. Pack the rucksack with the heavier things at the top, but with the needs for the day accessible. Right: A 'wild' backpack camp in the Pyrenean foothills

was done only after his camp was shipshape and everything was ready for cooking the evening meal. There was water to be fetched in the polythene bottle, the billy to be filled, his ground mat and other belongings to be laid out inside the tent, the materials for supper placed ready and the sleeping bag brought in when the shadow of the crag ended its airing in the sun. And when he set off on his exploration he zipped up the tent with everything inside it; there could be wandering sheep-dogs up here, and even sheep themselves had been known to nose into tents and spoil a supper.

It was dusk when he returned from admiring the sunset on a neighbouring hilltop, but there was enough light left to cook by. Once again he marvelled at how delicious vegetable soup from a packet could taste after a day's backpacking, and how greatly the flavour of biscuits and jam was improved when you ate the food sitting in your tent doorway with the wild upland landscape before you darkening with the coming of night. A last cup of coffee, and then he strolled over to the glimmering stream. There was gravel at its verge, just the stuff for scouring out the billy before a final swill with hot water. He had a wash and brushed his teeth; then — from a pool farther upstream — filled the billy ready for the morning. Now he was ready to turn in.

The night air was chill up here on the edge of the moorland, but in the zipped-up tent it was snug. He lit his candle in the holder on the tent pole and slid it up out of his way while he undressed. He never slept in the clothes he had been walking in — they were damp with body-moisture and made him cold in the small hours. He got into pyjamas and into the sleeping bag, then spent some time folding his clothes loosely into a comfortable pillow. Then he got out his log, the notebook in which he invariably set down the events of the day — something he would read again at home to recapture this holiday — and by the light of the candle he wrote it up to date.

When this was done he made his final preparations for the night. Boots ready by the door in case he had to get out in the night and the grass was wet with dew. It might well be cold later on though he was warm enough now, so he put his woollen sweater and jacket where he could reach them, and after consideration decided to put on a pair of socks — the spares, not the ones he had worn that day — to insure himself against cold feet. A last adjustment of the pillow, and he closed the zip of the sleeping bag and got himself comfortable with the bag pulled well up over the back of his head. He was asleep before there was time for a further thought.

8 Backpacking Routes of the World

The world offers innumerable possibilities for backpacking journeys; this chapter will give you an idea of the kind of routes you can follow. Some countries, those in South America and the Far East for example, demand the use of pack animals if long journeys are to be made through remote areas, and this sort of travel is outside the scope of this book. A journey through the magnificent Himalayan foothills, perhaps the finest tramp-camping terrain in the world, still requires local porters and a guide — and a working knowledge of Urdu. The summary that follows, therefore, is a collection of ideas for the ordinary backpacker looking for a place where his boots and his tent can be used with advantage and interest. On many of the routes mentioned, I have carried a pack myself and in these cases a brief note based on my experience is added.

Britain

In England and Wales there are ten national parks, and though day-walking from a base is the usual way of exploring them, the

Below: Part of the backpacker's way across Wales from north to south. Cader Idris in background

Above: Passes like the Bonderchrinde — the notch in the skyline — offer an invitation which the adventurous backpacker in the Bernese Oberland can accept. Below left: Coast path backpacking can provide quiet and beautiful campsites but fresh water will usually have to be fetched from the nearest dwelling

backpacker can work out longer routes using the park areas. I spent a week crossing the Lake District from Shap to the coast at Seascale, traversing the higher summits en route. A very worthwhile journey might also be made across England from west to east through the Lake District into the Yorkshire Dales National Park and finishing by the Cleveland Way long-distance footpath. Similarly, a north-south crossing of Snowdonia National Park makes a backpacking week, and can also begin a fine three-week journey right down to the most southerly point of Wales, Breaksea Point, bearing eastward through the wilds of the Black Mountain to avoid the coal-mining valleys. When I did this journey, I made for Gower instead of finishing the course, and spent the last two days following the cliffy coast of that delightful peninsula.

The twelve long-distance footpaths of England and Wales total over fifteen hundred miles of good walking, but not all of them are suitable for backpacking. On those of the South Country, you tread rather too close to the urban lifestyle for freedom, and on the six coastal footpaths (the longest is the Pembrokeshire Coast Path, 167 miles) it isn't easy to find a campsite every night or to locate safe drinking-water. The Pennine Way, longest and best known of the long-distance paths, is a good one for the backpacker. The two hundred and fifty miles from Edale in Derbyshire to Kirk Yetholm in Scotland took me seventeen days in 1965. Since then, the Way has become rather too 'well-beaten' and some of its best campsites are not as sanitary as they used to be. However, it's still an excellent route.

For information on national parks and long-distance footpaths, inquire at the Countryside Commission, St Anne's Gate, London W1, about the current brochure guides available.

Scotland has some wonderful backpacking country, but in general the journeys are more demanding unless you keep off the mountains. In the national forest parks, especially in the Glen Trool Park (Galloway), journeys of two or three days are rewarding, and in spite of road development, the careful planner can still make his way up the west coast with some backpacking freedom. But Torridon and Wester Ross, or the crossing of Badenoch and Lochaber, seventy miles of wild mountains crossed by only three roads, are routes for experienced mountain walkers. The Western Isles make unusual routes for the backpacker, and I recommend a journey I did a few years ago: down the Kintyre Peninsula, across to Islay and round its deserted coast, then on to the wilds of Jura. This trip made a memorable fortnight.

Norway

On none of my seven visits to Norway did I encounter anyone backpacking, though the tourist huts and trails in the Jotunheim are well frequented. Apart from two exploratory treks in Arctic Norway (where backpacking is the only way of travelling), I have always used *saeter* huts and remote farms for overnight shelter.

71

But a backpacking route going north from Bergen as far as Aalesund would make an original and unforgettable trip. There would be a lot of fjord-crossing by boat, and good map-reading would be essential because of the lack of signposted routes. Camping is unrestricted but it is illegal to make an open fire in forested country. The best time of year to go is mid-June to mid-July — not earlier because mountain trails may be under snow until the middle of June. August is a wet month in Norway. When planning a route, you can obtain advice from the Norwegian National Tourist Office, 20 Pall Mall, London SW1Y 5NE.

France

France has recently established more than four thousand miles of long-distance footpaths. These are called *Sentiers de Grande Randonnée;* they are carefully signposted and marked with the characteristic red and white waymark. In the main, these routes seem to be easy-going and rural. They are all numbered. By GR36, for instance, you will be able to walk from the coast of Britanny right across France to Banyuls on the Mediterranean. Normally walkers on these trails use hostels, inns, or one of the occasional official campsites, but the backpacker should have no difficulty in finding less sophisticated sites for his tent, particularly in areas like the Cevennes, Auvergne, and the Landes, three of the nineteen national and regional parks. Best of all for the mountain-minded backpacker are the GR paths in the French and Maritime Alps, on which you can walk south from Chamonix through the Vanoise and Dauphiné and end up at Nice. I have done part of this route and it is very fine indeed.

As usual in France, the sections of path are under the control of the local *Syndicat d'Initiatif* and detailed information has to be obtained directly from them. But an intending GR backpacker should obtain the ramblers' guidebooks called *topoguides* from the Comité National des Sentiers de Grande Randonnée, 65 Avenue de la Grande Armée, Paris 75016.

Germany

The home of the *Wandervögel* is naturally well provided with established walking routes; there are seventy-five thousand miles of marked footpaths, chiefly in the central uplands, which are fairly populous in summer with day-walkers and parties. There is usually a tavern or a restaurant not far away; this is walking country for backpackers who don't want to get too far away from 'civilization'! In the spring, the Bavarian valleys are lovely, though at that time of year the mountain routes must be avoided. The Black Forest and the Harz Mountains, the Schwabian Alb and the Odenwald north of Heidelberg, are a few of the regions where one could make a week's or a fortnight's backpacking journey. The Black Forest footpaths reach far, and the *Hohenweg* from Pforzheim to Basle (217 miles) must be a fine route. Another grand journey for those whose preference is for historic scenery and romantic castles rather than for wild open country would be the footpath route down the Rhine, especially at the vintage time. Walking can be varied with brief spells on the down-river tourist ships. I think my own choice for a journey with pack and tent — perhaps because I have walked parts of it — would be southern Germany, where Bavaria meets the Austrian Tyrol. Here you can find those beautiful and solitary campsites which are the backpacker's joy, and vary the valleys and easy passes with hair-raising paths on the rocky crests, if you feel like it. The Allgäu and Berchtesgaden Alps have superb scenery which only the wanderer afoot can see, and since the mountains are not high you can get right on to them without crossing snow and glaciers.

Regional associations maintain the paths, as in France, and there are numerous official campsites. The central association for these *Rundwanderwegen* is the Verband Deutscher Gebirgs und Wanderverein, D7 Stuttgart 1, Hospitalstrasse 21b, Germany, but for preliminary information in Britain it would be advisable to write first to the German Tourist Information Bureau, 61 Conduit Street, London W1.

Austria
Just south of the German frontier there is a stretch of grand backpacking country. Mountain areas don't change a great deal over the years, and I have no doubt that the valleys of the Karwendel and Rofan are still as magnificent as they were when I walked there in 1962. To backpack through these spectacular ranges is an adventure, but with milder alternatives; there are good huts if the weather gets too bad for enjoyable camping, and the marked paths on the rock crests can be varied by easier ways round at a lower level. Here is the outline of one good route, for a trip lasting a week or ten days: from Scharnitz in the Isar valley north of Innsbruck traverse the Karwendel eastward, over the Holjoch into the Eng, out over the Plumserjoch or Falzthurnalm, down to Pertisau on the Achensee; then from the south end of the Achensee, traverse the Rofangebirge via the Spieljoch, Bettlersteigsattel, and Rofan; then down to Schaffsteigsattel and over Sagzahn and Vorderer Sonnwendjoch; then from a camp by the delightful Zireinensee over the low pass to Ampmoosboden, finishing with a descent to Steinberg. The route could also be continued eastward from Steinberg, perhaps to finish at Salzburg.

The mountains of the Tyrol — Oetztal, Stubai, and the Zillertal Alps — are high and snow-covered, but there is nothing to prevent a stout-hearted backpacker from making a journey along the frontier ranges between Austria and Italy, camping in the valley-heads of the Tyrol and crossing the passes from one to another. The paths are well marked and very scenic, taking you through the heart of some of the finest scenery in Europe. The Austrian huts are famous for their size and near-hotel luxury and there is usually

one on or near a main pass, though the dedicated backpacker will scorn their use (except, maybe, for a *stein* of lager) and find his ideal campsites in the upper valleys. Some easy snow will have to be crossed, but though I took an ice axe on my own fourteen-day journey through the Oetztal and Stubai ranges, a stout staff would have served just as well. A summary of that journey may give some idea of Tyrolean travel: first camp at Huben in the lower Oetztal (reached by bus from Innsbruck); cross the Breitlehner Jochl into Pitztal; Pitztaler Jochl into Rettenbach valley; from camp at Vent, over Ramol Jochl down to Obergurgl; camp above Solden in Oetztal; cross Atterkar Jochl (snow) into upper Sulztal; over Mutterberger Jochl and down Mutterbergertal to Ranalt; camp above Neustift; up Pinnistal to Innsbrucker Hut and down to Gschnitz; over Muttenjochl to Obernberg and finish at Gries on the Brenner road. Another fortnight of superb mountain tramping could be added by continuing east from this point through the Zillertal valleys.

The excellent Austrian 1:100,000 maps covering these ranges (*Freytag-Berndt* Sheets 15, 24, 25) show all the paths and marked routes; from these maps many other journeys can be planned. Inquiries can be made to the Austrian National Tourist Office, 16 Conduit Street, London W1R 0AL.

The Alps
It is now recognized that the backpacker has enormous opportunities in the Alps — the greatest of European mountain massifs. Between the high peaks where only the mountaineer can go and the valley roads where the tourist cars swarm there is a network of high-level tracks which take the walker through the grandest alpine scenery without requiring the use of rope or ice axe. By using these tracks to link the passes under ten thousand feet, pausing in the valley centres only to stock up for the next three camps, and pitching the tent wherever fresh water and a breathtaking view invite you to stop, you can make unforgettable backpacking journeys. As examples, I give brief outlines of two Alpine backpacking journeys I made recently, the Bernese Oberland traverse in 1972, and the Valais Alps in 1974.

Bernese Oberland We made a west-to-east traverse of the range, taking three weeks, from Montreux to Meiringen. Starting from Bex near Montreux, we headed for Gsteig over Col des Essets, Pas de Cheville, and Col du Sanetsch; thence by the Krinnen, Truttlisberg, and Hahnenmoos passes to Adelboden. We went into the Engstligen Alp to gain the Gemmi Pass by way of the Kindbetti path and the Rote Kumme, down the Gemmi to Leukerbad and by the Resti and Lötschen Passes to Kandersteg. Then we went to Lauterbrunnen over the Hohtürli and the Sefinenfurgge (the former, at 9,114ft, was the highest on the route) and finally crossed Kleine Scheidegg and Grosse Scheidegg to finish at Meiringen. Official campsites at Gsteig, Adelboden, Lauterbrunnen and

Grindelwald were used; otherwise, the tent was pitched 'wild' in mountain nooks. Ascents on this scenic and varied route totalled just over forty thousand feet. In the first section, some route-finding was required; from Gsteig onwards, the paths were well waymarked. (Maps: *Carte Nationale de la Suisse* Sheets 272, 273, 263, 264.)

Valais Alps Again we made a west-to-east traverse, taking three weeks, from Martigny to the Simplon. We started from Verbier above Martigny, went via the Louvie, Prafleuri, and Riedmatten Cols to Arolla, down the valley to Les Haudères, and across Col de Torrent, Col de Sorebois, and Col de Forcletta to Gruben in the Turtmanntal. Thence we went over Augstbord Pass to St Niklaus and by the high-level path from the Täsch Alp to Zermatt (there was a good 'wild' campsite by the Grindjisee above Zermatt). Then we went down again to St Niklaus for the crossing of the easy Hannig Pass to Saas Fée, and thence over the high Simeli Pass and Bistinen Pass to the Simplon road and Brig. An easy alternative to the Simeli is the Gebidem Pass farther north. Only one official site was used, at Saas Fée; the other nineteen camps were pitched in wild and beautiful surroundings. Paths are well waymarked except on the Simeli Pass. (Maps: *Carte Nationale de la Suisse* Sheets 283, 284, 273, 274.) Inquiries should be made at the Swiss National Tourist Office, 1 New Coventry Street, London W1V 3HG.

Other backpacking routes in the Alps worth considering are the circuit round Mont Blanc, starting from Chamonix and using the Cols of Bonhomme, Seigne, Ferret, D'Arpette, and Balme to circle in and out of Italy and return to Chamonix; and the Dolomite High Routes, high-level paths through the spectacular northern Italian mountains.

Spain

Unusual and rewarding backpacking journeys can be made in the Picos de Europa of Cantabria or among the Sierra of the south (though in summer the latter would be rather hot for walking), but the Spanish Pyrenees provide what is in my opinion the most free and satisfying backpacking in Europe. On the French side of the range, roads and sophisticated tourist centres come too close to the frontier for really free walking, but on the Spanish side the mountains are still extraordinarily remote and very beautiful. In July and August of 1973, I made a four-week journey here with three companions, camping wild every night and crossing eight passes, with exploratory trips into the outlying ranges, such as the Sierra de las Encantadas. We met a few climbers heading for the peaks, but no other walkers. We stocked up every three or four days at high Spanish villages, and though such things as *Camping Gaz* were rarely obtainable, plentiful supplies of firewood were available. Access to this lovely country is easy: train to Luchon or Ax-les-Thermes on the French side in twenty-one hours from London, and on the first day you cross your first Pyrenean pass

Above: Up the mule-track after stocking-up in the valley (Pyrenees)

into Spain or Andorra. There is little waymarking on the paths, but these are usually old mule tracks and are not hard to follow. Spanish tourist offices know little of backpacking routes, but handy guidebooks to the mountains (in French) are published by the *Centre Excursioniste de Catalogne.* These and the relevant Spanish maps can be obtained through Gastons Alpine Bookshop, 134 Kenton Road, Harrow, Middlesex.

The United States

Influential groups such as the Sierra Club have initiated the present construction and extension of the network of national scenic trails, and there are now at least sixteen of these criss-crossing the USA from east to west and north to south. Some of them are much used, but a recent survey revealed that no less than ninety-five per cent of walkers stick to the same five per cent of trails, so the backpacker who wants to avoid crowds can choose from many picturesque and well-maintained paths through some of the finest scenery in the world. The two longest and best routes are the Appalachian Trail in the east and the Pacific Crest Trail in the west.

The Appalachian Trail With a length of about two thousand miles, running from Mount Katahdin in Maine to Springer Mountain in Georgia, this trail traverses fourteen states. It is carefully waymarked and well provided with facilities for walkers. Every mile has been measured and marked; the waymarks may be metal tags, tree-blazes in forest, or small cairns in open country. Open-faced shelters and lean-tos are spaced along the trail at regular intervals, and other closed shelters belonging to local

Appalachian Trail clubs can be used for a small payment. However, it is still advisable to take a lightweight tent, especially in holiday periods on popular parts of the route. Journeys on the Appalachian Trail are in every way easier than on the Pacific Crest Trail. The highest point reached on the Appalachian Trail is 6,641ft at Clingman's Dome in the Great Smoky Mountains of the Pisgah National Forest. A booklet, *The Appalachian Trail* (publication 17) and other information can be obtained from the Appalachian Trail Conference, 1718 N. Street N.W., Washington, D.C.

The Pacific Crest Trail This journey through the mountains from the Canadian frontier to the Mexican frontier is the backpacking trip of a lifetime. The total of 2,313 miles was first walked continuously by eighteen-year-old Eric Ryback in 1970. Trail crews of the Forest Service are still working on some parts of the route where direction-finding is difficult; eventually there will be a beaten track throughout its length. The trail traverses nineteen major canyons, passes some nine hundred lakes, and crosses fifty-seven high mountain passes. There are Forest Guard stations or government camps here and there, but they do not provide supplies; the backpacker must be prepared to support himself for five days between valley supply points, and to encounter bears, skunks, and porcupines — all of which must be left alone. Because the route climbs to well over ten thousand feet at many points, no part of it should be tackled before July, and the first snows may render these high sections difficult or impassable as early as September.

A backpacker from Europe with some mountain walking experience and a month's vacation would do well to choose the section called the John Muir Trail for his journey. He would need to be tough, for this 178-mile trail passes through the Rockies where the highest peaks are grouped — three hundred and six of them over twelve thousand feet. The John Muir Trail begins in Yosemite National Park and the start of the journey, which would take twenty to twenty-five days, should be not earlier than late July, to avoid being stopped by late-lying snow. As it passes into Sequoia National Park, the John Muir Trail climbs over Forester's Pass, at 13,200ft, 'the highest pass for man and beast in the USA', so even in August warm clothing or proper mountain clothes are required. For this and other journeys on the Pacific Crest, maps and information on route conditions and weather should be obtained from the Forest Service Pacific Northwest, Regional Office, P.O. Box 3623, Portland, Oregon 97212, USA.

In a territory as vast as the United States there are obviously other opportunities for backpacking journeys, both long and short. Among the longer and tougher of them is the journey right through the Grand Canyon of the Colorado River, which Colin Fletcher took two months to complete. Fletcher's book *The Man Who Walked Through Time* is a backpacking classic and a mine of practical information for all who tramp with a pack.

9 Tips and Gimmicks

Boot lacing For maximum foot comfort, pull the laces only just taut on the three hooks or eyelets nearest the toe on each boot, and lace the rest good and tight.

Camp fire tips (1) If you're using a fire for cooking, be sure to cover the fireplace with a flat rock before turning in; a fire lights more quickly on dry ground. (2) Blowing-up a sulky fire is an easy job if you're in wooded country where elder grows. Three feet of green elder-stick with the pith extracted makes a good blow-pipe. (3) Genuine hoboes have used hot rocks for centuries to keep themselves warm at night. Large round stones placed amid the embers for an hour or so retain their warmth all night — but don't put a hot rock on a nylon groundsheet!

Containers The little canisters used for packing 35mm camera film make useful containers for salt, tablets, safety-pins, buttons, or matches. Matches can be further waterproofed by dipping them for half their length in shellac varnish thinned with alcohol, and then drying them separately on a sheet of paper.

Dental care If your toothbrush gets left at a campsite, or you forget both brush and toothpaste when packing, don't worry. If you've packed the salt, that makes a safe and effective tooth-powder, and a hazel twig frayed out at one end is an efficient brush.

Diet A man requires a minimum intake of 1700 calories per day, which can be produced by a diet containing roughly fifty per cent carbohydrates, twenty-five to thirty per cent protein, and twenty to twenty-five per cent fats. For the backpacking diet enthusiast, here are some approximate calorie-producing values per three and a half ounces of weight:

Black or rye bread — 250 calories
Muesli cereal — 300 calories
Sweets — 400 calories
Eggs — 600 calories
Cheese — 300 calories
Butter — 700 calories
Jam — 270 calories
Sweet biscuits — 400 calories

Vitamins A, B1, and D are provided in these foods (an egg has them all) but not Vitamin C, which is provided by fresh fruit or a tomato.

Distance judging It's satisfactory, and could be useful on occasion, to be able to judge how far in front or behind your companion is. At eight hundred yards and over a moving man is just a dot. Between eight hundred and six hundred yards he becomes a vertical dark mark. Between six hundred and four hundred yards the movement of walking legs can be made out. Between four hundred and two hundred yards a face, but not features, can be seen.

locking a
metal runner

Family backpacking The arrival of a third member in a backpacking family will obviously interrupt holiday walking for a short while but needn't do so for more than a year. Even a toddler doesn't take up much room in a two-man tent. There are problems, of course, and overcoming them has to be looked upon as part of the fun. On the trail, mother can carry the child, while father carries everything else. This means a rather large and heavy pack, and a journey of short hauls in countryside that is not too steep and rough or too remote. The diaper problem is best solved by carrying disposables. A trial day trip can be taken using a home-made carrier for the child, such as an old rucksack with two leg-holes cut in the bottom, but for an actual backpacking journey a child must have a proper carrier like the *Papoose,* made by Karrimor. If you think backpacking's no sport for tender infants, remember that millions of babies have traditionally been carried like this.

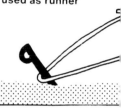

'tarbuck' knot
used as runner

Guy slides The metal runner on the guy-line has a notch in it so that it can be held in position. If you lose a runner, a Tarbuck knot on a loop is a good substitute — when pulled up tight the knot can be slid up and down the guy-line by hand, but it will grip if strain comes on the guy.

Above: Guy slides. Below: A map-measurer, useful for measuring distances by footpath or across trackless country

Hitch-hiking If three or four miles of main road has to be tramped between paths the backpacker may well think of trying a hitch.
Likely ways of *not* getting a lift are:
Lounging in the wayside grass and waving a thumb
Thumbing midway along a fast and busy stretch of road
Walking along and swinging a thumb without looking round
Thumbing in a bunch with three companions
Likely ways of succeeding are:
Thumbing close to a layby or pull-in
Facing the oncoming cars and looking gently beseeching
Showing your national flag on the pack if you're abroad
Being clean and tidy, with a smart and compact load

Insect repellent The cones or small candles which give off a fumigant smoke when lit are obtainable from camping stockists and are most effective both inside and outside the tent.

Knife One heavy knife in the party is worth its weight. A sheath-knife with a blade four and a half inches long and seven-eighths of an inch broad, of unbending steel, is best for all-round use. Camp picnic-type knives or penknives are useless, even dangerous, when used for cutting hard loaves or trimming a staff.

Litter 'If you pack it in, pack it out' is a backpacking rule. A large

plastic bag (takes up little room in the pack when empty and weighs next to nothing) is useful as a litter-repository in the tent and you can take *all* your rubbish in it to the first proper dumping-place you come to.

Map-measurer This item is handy when estimating walking distance on the map. The small traversing wheel records miles or kilometres on the dial.

Pillow 'A good soft pillow', according to Shakespeare, 'were better than a churlish turf', and most backpackers will agree. Rather than carrying an unsatisfactory air-pillow (which is never soft) most people contrive a pillow from clothing. Boots make a useful base for the pillow, placed on their sides with the uppers inwards and the toes uppermost, about fourteen inches apart. Folded nylon protective clothing goes on the boots, then thicker clothing, with a woollen sweater as the top surface. This system has the added advantage that you don't have to look far for your boots if you need them in the night: they're right under your nose.

Sanitary matters When camping 'wild', remember that human excreta must be buried six inches deep. A good big tuft of grass, lifted and replaced afterwards, will serve the purpose. The place should be at least fifty yards from camp, water, and path. Try not to use a place that might be picked by someone else for a tent site. Strong tissues can be used as toilet paper, among other things. They should be packed in a well-sealed plastic bag, such as a map-case with Velcro fastening.

Slimmers The phenomenon of a decreased waist measurement is reported by nearly all who do a backpacking journey of a week or more. For most of us this is highly satisfactory, but it can be awkward, towards the end of the journey, if your trousers or breeches depend on built-in belt or waistband. To avoid having to walk with one hand holding up the lower garments, it is a good idea to put extra holes in the belt or additional buttons where they might be needed.

Spare line An extra well worth the seven and a half ounces of additional weight is a ten metre length of perlon (or nylon) line. It can serve as a double storm-guy for the tent, a clothes-line, and a safeguard against unexpected hazards on steep routes.

Spare tent pegs Always carry at least three pegs over and above the total number used for the tent. They are easy things to lose, especially if you don't check the number every time you strike camp. Two of the spares will come in useful if you are pitched on poor peg-holding ground and a strong wind threatens to uproot one of the pole-guy pegs. This peg can be secured by putting in two more pegs behind it, so that the original peg is at the right-angle of a triangle of pegs. Pass a line taut from one support-peg round the original peg and tie back to the other. A small coil of stout string or cord should be carried in the ditty-bag for this sort of thing.

Swim trunks These can substitute as spare briefs and come in

handy on a hot day when a tempting pool is too near the path for privacy.

Tent lighting A candle is safe in a tent if used with care. My unpatented candle-holder, for use with a centre-pole tent, is made from two spring tool-clips (from any ironmonger), fastened back to back with a little nut-and-bolt through the screw-holes. One clip must be of a size to grip the pole firmly, the other to hold the candle. The wax-catcher is a plastic lid from a food jar, with a candle-diameter hole cut in it. To prevent the clips from swivelling, supplement the nut-and-bolt fastening with Araldite.

Tentpole linkage Light alloy poles in sections are sometimes a nuisance to assemble correctly in their proper sockets, particularly the three-piece poles. Some sets of poles come already linked. If they don't, you can provide your own linkage by drilling small holes just above the joint on each of the adjoining sections, taking care that the hole in the socket pole is clear of the point to which the push-in pole will come. Thread cord through the pairs of holes, knotting the inside ends with 'figure-of-eight' stopper knots. Allow just enough joining cord so that the joint can be made without straining the cord. The sections can still be packed side by side as before, but they will be ready for instant assembly without mistake, even in the dark.

Tip for the tip-over In a small tent mugs of tea do get tipped over sometimes. A sponge or square of foam-rubber comes in handy for these emergencies — you can mop up quickly and squeeze with one hand outside the tent door. My mug fits snugly into the top of a walking-boot, which is a much safer place for it than on the groundsheet.

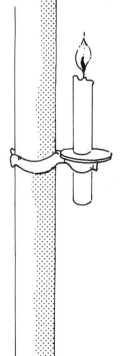

86

Tired feet A surprisingly effective remedy for this common ailment is simply to change-over socks and stockings from the left foot to the right and vice versa.

Previous page: The author, crossing the Resti Pass, on a backpacking traverse of the Bernese Oberland

Waist straps These are fitted to many packs as standard equipment. Some backpackers always wear them fastened, others never use them. They are most useful when carrying a high-loaded pack on steep and rugged ground, to prevent the pack from swinging sideways or even tipping right over your head. If you don't like waist straps, attach a pair of strong tapes or laces which can be left coiled on the packframe and brought into action when required.

Washing clothes When time, site, and weather suggest an hour or two spent in washing clothes the backpacker customarily takes a cold and soapy splash first, and then puts on fresh clothes. A smooth round rock on the verge of a pool makes an ideal scrubbing-board. With a two-tent party the washing line can be rigged between tentpoles. Clothes pegs can be made from nearby trees: green twigs half an inch in diameter are cut to about four inches in length and slit down one end about two inches. However, you won't need pegs if you have enough line to rig it double. Twist the double line fairly tightly throughout its length, and secure the ends. The washing then is held by passing the corners through a couple of twists. In rocky country, clothes will dry with amazing speed on sunwarmed boulders, but beware the sudden breeze that whisks them off and into the stream again. Weighted down with smaller rocks, they will stay put.

Water purifiers You are at risk drinking unpurified water unless it is from a mountain stream with no dwellings higher up its course. Doubtful water should always be boiled before use; but an overnight test will tell you whether you can safely drink it unboiled. Place a lump or a spoonful of granulated sugar in a mug of water and let it stand overnight. If the water turns milky, it is impure and unfit to drink. Water-purifying tablets remove all risk but leave an unpleasant taste in the water. To minimize this taste, put the purifier in the water-bottle, shake very vigorously with the top on for a full minute, then remove the top and let the water stand for five minutes before drinking. If your taste-buds still revolt, your only remedy is to add lemonade powder.

APPENDIX

British suppliers
Backpacking equipment

There are many other firms supplying equipment in addition to those named below, which are listed to give wide regional coverage.

Berghaus
34 Dean Street
Newcastle-upon-Tyne NE1 1PG

Blacks of Greenock
Port Glasgow
Renfrewshire PA14 5XN

Brown Best & Co Ltd
47 Old Woolwich Road
London SE10 9PU

Bukta
Brinksway
Stockport
Cheshire SK4 1ED

Field & Trek Ltd
25 Kings Road
Brentwood
Essex

Karrimor
Avenue Road
Accrington
Lancs BB5 6PR

MOAC
Liverpool Road
Manchester M34 4NQ

Pindisports
14 Holborn
London EC1

Pindisports
27/29 Martinean Street
Birmingham

Robert Saunders
Chigwell
Essex

Ultimate Equipment Ltd
Warksworth
Morpeth
Northumberland

Vango (Scotland) Ltd
356 Amulree Street
Glasgow C2

YHA Services Ltd
London: 29 John Adam Street WC2N 6JE
Manchester: 36/38 Fountain Street M2 2BE
Birmingham: 35 Cannon Street B2 5EE

Compasses
Silva Compasses London Ltd
76 Broad Street
Teddington
Middlesex TW11 8QT

Backpacking foods
Springlow Sales Ltd
Marsland Industrial Estate
Werneth
Oldham, Lancs

Swel Foods Ltd
Dawnedge
Apsley Guise, Bletchley
Bucks

USA suppliers
Backpacking equipment

Fabiano Shoe Co Inc
South Boston
Mass 02127

Holubar Mountaineering Ltd
Boulder
Colorado 80302

Kelty
Glendale
California 91201

Mountain Products Corporation
Wenatchee
Wash 98807

Recreational Equipment Inc
Seattle
Wash 98122

Backpacking foods
Rich-Moor
Van Nuys
California 91404

Mountain House
Albany
Oregon 97321

Key packing list

This list is comprehensive and includes items which individual backpackers will leave out according to their needs and tastes.

To go in the pack
tent with sewn-in groundsheet
poles and pegs
flysheet
ground mat
sleeping bag
stove
spare gaz cylinder
two billies
deep plate

frypan
knife
fork
spoons
can-opener
sheath knife
wool sweater
pyjamas
spare vest
spare briefs
spare stockings
spare socks
tent slippers
shorts
swim trunks

Ditty-bag containing:
   razor or battery shaver
   plastic shopping-bag
   candle-holder
   candles
   ten-metre line
   matches
   glucose tablets (reserve)
   handkerchiefs
   personal medicines
   camera film

Hussif containing:
   needle and thread
   darning needle and wool
   buttons
   finger bandages
   safety pins
   scissors
   antiseptic ointment
   self-adhesive pvc tape
   moleskin

cagoule
overtrousers

towel
soap
comb
toothbrush
toothpaste
nailbrush
tissues in plastic case

salt
sugar
three packet soups
tea
coffee
milk powder
To go in pack pockets
maps
compass
notebook
pencil
mug
sweets
chocolate
camera
hat

To go in jacket pockets for travel
money
tickets
passport
travellers cheques

Additions for winter backpacking
To go in the pack
heavy instead of light wool sweater
woollen balaclava
wool gloves
windproof outer mitts
double layer ground mat or three quarter length airbed
torch and batteries
To wear
heavy woollen shirt
proofed cotton anorak or lined jacket
thick natural fibre trousers or breeches

If journeying in snow-covered hills, wear pvc gaiters and
carry an ice axe in place of a staff.

FURTHER READING

Books
Belloc, Hilaire *The Path to Rome* Nelson
Bradt, H. and G. *Backpacking Along Ancient Ways in
   Peru and Bolivia* Bradt Enterprises, Boston
Davies, Hunter *A Walk Along The Wall* Weidenfeld &
   Nicolson
Fletcher, Colin *The Man Who Walked Through Time*
   Knopf
Graham, Stephen *The Gentle Art of Tramping* Holden
Hillaby, John *Journey Through Britain* Constable
Hillaby, John *Journey Through Europe* Constable
Pyatt, Edward C. *Coastal Paths Of The South West*
   David & Charles
Rethmel, Robert C. *Backpacking* Burgess USA

Handbooks available from YHA Services Ltd
Camping and Hill Trekking Pelham
Coastal Paths Of The South West David & Charles
Colour Photography Penguin
Lightweight Camping Lutterworth Press
Offa's Dyke Shell Guides
Orienteering Faber
Rambling and Lightweight Camping Countrygoer Books
Recipes for Campers Hostellers and Caravanners
   Dalesman
Safety and First Aid Pan
South Downs Way Spur
The Cleveland Way HMSO
The Pennine Way HMSO
The Sea Shore Fontana
The Weather Guide Hamlyn
Wild Flowers Hamlyn

Magazine
The Climber and Rambler Monthly

INDEX

Numbers in italics refer to captions to illustrations